Passing the Principal as Instructional Leader TExES Exam

Third Edition

This third edition of Passing the Principal as Instructional Leader TExES Exam: Keys to Certification and School Leadership *remains dedicated to my beloved husband of 46 years, Greg Wilmore; our children, Brandon Greggory Wilmore and Brooke Elaine Wilmore; our daughter Brittani Wilmore Rollen, her awesome husband, Ryan, and their brilliant and beautiful children, Blair Elaine and Lucas Ryan; my late parents Lee and Irene Watson Litchfield; my oldest and dearest friend in the world who has put up with me our entire lives, Melda Cole Ward, and all my other friends, colleagues, and students who love and pray for me when I least deserve it. Thank you for being the wind beneath my wings and for always encouraging me to get back up when I fall down. I love you all.*

*"For I know the **plans** I have for you," declares the Lord, "plans to* **prosper** *you and not to harm you, plans to give you **hope** and a **future**.*

*Then you will **call upon me** and **come and pray to me**, and I will **listen** to you.*

You will seek me and find me when you seek me with all your heart."

Jeremiah 29: 11–13

*I can do **all** things through Christ who*

strengthens me*.*

Philippians 4:13

Passing the Principal as Instructional Leader TExES Exam

Keys to Certification and School Leadership

Third Edition

Elaine L. Wilmore
Foreword by Jeanne M. Gerlach

FOR INFORMATION:

Corwin

A SAGE Company

2455 Teller Road

Thousand Oaks, California 91320

(800) 233-9936

www.corwin.com

SAGE Publications Ltd.

1 Oliver's Yard

55 City Road

London EC1Y 1SP

United Kingdom

SAGE Publications India Pvt. Ltd.

B 1/I 1 Mohan Cooperative Industrial Area

Mathura Road, New Delhi 110 044

India

SAGE Publications Asia-Pacific Pte. Ltd.

18 Cross Street #10-10/11/12

China Square Central

Singapore 048423

Publisher: Arnis Burvikovs

Development Editor: Desirée A. Bartlett

Senior Editorial Assistant: Eliza Erickson

Production Editor: Amy Schroller

Copy Editor: Deanna Noga

Typesetter: C&M Digitals (P) Ltd.

Proofreader: Theresa Kay

Indexer: Terri Morrissey

Cover Designer: Scott Van Atta

Marketing Manager: Sharon Pendergast

Printed in the United States of America

Library of Congress Cataloging-in-Publication Data

Names: Wilmore, Elaine L., author.

Title: Passing the Principal as Instructional Leader TExES Exam : keys to certification and school leadership / Elaine L. Wilmore ; foreword by Jeanne M. Gerlach, Ed.D., Ph.D., Associate Provost for K-16 Initiatives, The University of Texas at Arlington.

Description: Third Edition. | Thousand Oaks, California : CORWIN, A SAGE Company, [2019] | Includes bibliographical references and index.

Identifiers: LCCN 2018042303 | ISBN 9781544342153 (Paperback : acid-free paper)

Subjects: LCSH: School principals—Certification—Texas. | Educational tests and measurements—Texas.

Classification: LCC LB1769.T49 W58 2019 | DDC 371.2/01209764—dc23

LC record available at https://lccn.loc.gov/2018042303

This book is printed on acid-free paper.

19 20 21 22 23 10 9 8 7 6 5 4 3 2 1

Contents

SECTION IV AFTER YOU PASS THE TEST: THAT'S WHAT IT'S ALL ABOUT!

Foreword

Elaine Wilmore is yet again serving our prospective principals by publishing a third edition of her overwhelmingly successful *Passing the Principal as Instructional Leader TExES Exam: Keys to Certification and School Leadership*. Here in the third volume, Dr. Wilmore offers information to help students pass the all-new exam. With clear and coherent writing, she offers a one-of-a-kind guide that, like her other books, will undoubtedly become the Gold Standard of test-taking manuals.

This edition is truly an accessible and authentic read. Describing the six domains and eleven competencies that are included on the exam but with careful attention to the new additions, Wilmore offers practical and detailed information that will assist any student to pass the challenging TExES exam. The first editions of the book were used or recommended by most universities in Texas, and those who have used the book sing its praises and recommend it to their colleagues.

Elaine Wilmore's books have kept her on the Corwin Best Seller List and the Corwin Million Dollar Seller List. This edition promises to do the same.

Passing the Principal as Instructional Leader TExES Exam is a must read for anyone thinking about taking the TExES principal's exam. Elaine Wilmore's book is an example of an author whose writing is serving the next generation of K–12 school leaders.

Jeanne M. Gerlach, PhD, EdD
The University of Texas at Arlington
Associate Provost for K–16 Initiatives

Preface

*P*assing the Principal as Instructional Leader TExES Exam: Keys to Certification and School Leadership was written to help educators in Texas pass the principal Texas Examinations of Educator Standards (TExES). The original 2002 edition became an instant Corwin best seller, and the second edition remains a best seller to this day. It is used by universities and alternative preparation programs, as well as individual students, across the state. This third edition is based on six new domains and eleven competencies provided through Texas law (19 Texas Administrative Code Chapter 241.15) and developed by the Texas State Board for Educator Certification (SBEC) and the success of the two original editions. It is written based on the years of experience Wilmore has as a teacher, counselor, principal, professor, and school board member as well as providing popular, successful, and inspiring TExES preparation seminars and webinars at universities, regional service centers, and other training sites around the state. In addition, this updated version addresses the changes from the 068 version of the TExES to the new 268 version.

The nature of the book is both broad and specific. Part I provides the global overview, tools, and format of the book. Part II provides the philosophy and theoretical framework for TExES success. It details the Texas domains, competencies, and leadership philosophy on which TExES is constructed. Each of Part II's eleven chapters details a specific competency in a down-to-earth, interesting manner using real-life stories for practical application while engaging the reader and connecting theory to practice. Each chapter has the details necessary for proactive school leadership and TExES success. The book closes with an extensive list of additional resources to supplement each domain. Section III ties the philosophy of TExES to other important test-taking concepts and techniques such as how to read and analyze data, manage time while testing, and use specific strategies to discern correct answers. It includes information about how to create an individualized personal success plan, how to prepare for the TExES, and what to do in the weeks, days, and night before the test.

Passing the Principal as Instructional Leader TExES Exam: Keys to Certification and School Leadership, third edition is a valued asset for current administrators seeking to refine, refocus, and develop their learner-centered leadership skills as well as helping aspiring administrators pass the TExES examination. With a proven record of success, the book not only provides a solid theoretical framework for school leadership, it will make learning fun and inspire greatness. Readers will enjoy the book, be ready to pass the TExES exam, and then to change the world—one school at a time.

Acknowledgments

God has blessed me with such a wonderful family and so many great friends. It is simply impossible to acknowledge them all for everything they have brought to my life. My books come from my heart and my faith as a gift to others. Without my family, friends, and my faith, where would my heart be? What would it hold?

So, in the simplest of words, thank you. Thank you to my husband, Greg, to our children Brandon and Brooke Wilmore, Brittani and Ryan Rollen, and our beautiful and brilliant grandchildren, Blair Elaine and Lucas Ryan. Thank you to my friends who always surround me with love and support. It would be absolutely impossible to name you all, but here are a few: all my family, particularly my beloved sister, Marlene Litchfield Carter and her brave husband, Bill Carter. Marlene suffered a stroke 2 years ago, but she continues to fight courageously. I love her and am so very proud of her; my two goddaughters, Katharyn Davis and Celeste Arnold; Dr. Joe and Kathy Martin, JoNell and Larry Jones, Dottie and Ken, Betsy Ruffin, Brenda and Gregg Gammon, Kerry Van Dorin Pedigo, and our beloved Ruidoso pastor, Dr. Alan Stoddard, who always encourages us to stay "stoked up" for Jesus. Last, but definitely not least, a huge thank you to my lifelong beloved soulmate Melda Cole Ward who has stood by me through thick and thin for our entire lives. Few are blessed with the quality and quantity of my family and friends. I am truly blessed.

I must always thank my parents, the late Lee and Irene Litchfield, to whom I owe all that I am or ever will be. They taught me values, faith, a sense of humor, and to love and care for others. They were old-fashioned conservative parents who protected me until the days they went to be with Jesus. They also always supported my lifelong love of reading, libraries, and all things related to books. I miss you both so much. We will be together again someday in heaven. When that day comes, we will rock that place!

Love always,
Elaine

"... saying, I am Alpha and Omega, the first and the last: and, what thou seest, write in a book, ..." Revelation 1:11

About the Author

Elaine L. Wilmore, PhD, teaches online for the University of Texas of the Permian Basin and is also the owner of Elaine L. Wilmore Leadership Initiatives. She formerly served as Chair of Educational Leadership at Texas A&M at Texarkana, Texas A&M at Commerce, and Professor, Chair of Educational Leadership, Counseling, and Foundations as well as Doctoral Director at the University of Texas of the Permian Basin. She has previously served at Dallas Baptist University as Assistant Vice President for Educational Networking and Program Director for the MEd and EdD degrees in Educational Leadership. She has formerly served as special assistant to the Dean for NCATE Accreditation, Chair and Associate Professor of Educational Leadership and Policy Studies at the University of Texas at Arlington, President of the National Council of Professors of Educational Administration, President of the Texas Council of Professors of Educational Administration, and president of the Board of Trustees of the Cleburne Independent School District where she served for 9 years. She is the founding director of the Dallas Baptist University EdD in Educational Leadership and multiple programs at the University of Texas at Arlington (UTA) including all initial programs, Educational Leadership UTA, and the Scholars of Practice Program. While at UTA, she was also principal investigator for multiple grants for innovative field-based principal preparation programs. She has served as Director of University Program Development at UTA where she also developed and was the original Chair of the Faculty Governance Committee for the College of Education. Dr. Wilmore is professionally active and has served on many local, state, and national boards. These include having served on the Executive Committee of the National Council Professors of Educational Administration, the American Educational Research Association Executive Committee on the Teaching in Educational Administration SIG, the Texas Principals Leadership Initiative, the Texas Consortium of Colleges of Teacher Education, and as a program/folio reviewer for the Educational Leadership Constituent Council. She holds the unique distinction of being one of the few to have served as both a private and public school district Board of Trustees member.

Dr. Wilmore is honored to be on the Corwin "Best Seller" List and last year to have been named a "Million Dollar Book Seller," awards she is incredibly humbled by.

Dr. Wilmore was a public school teacher, counselor, elementary, and middle school principal before she moved to higher education. In addition to her significant work in educational leadership, assessment, and program development, she enjoys reading, writing, walking, traveling, music, and spending time with those she loves. She is the wife of Greg Wilmore; the only child of her late beloved parents, Lee and Irene Litchfield; the mother of three wonderful children, Brandon Greggory Wilmore, Brooke Elaine Wilmore, and Brittani Leigh Wilmore Rollen; and has a fabulous son-in-law, Ryan Rollen. Top highlights of her life are her grandchildren, Miss Blair Elaine Rollen and Mr. Lucas Ryan Rollen. Newer beloved additions to her life are her goddaughters, Celeste Arnold and Katharyn Davis. Elaine has three geriatric, yet still outstanding Pug dogs, named Annabella Rose, Isabella Lace, and Tug the Pug, plus two Boxers, Bridgette Elise and Sassi Abigail, that she loves dearly. In her limited spare time she dreams of learning to play the violin, viola, and cello and also of taking leisurely hot, peach bubble baths by candlelight in Italy.

SECTION I

Content

The Knowledge Base

CHAPTER 1
Welcome!

iStock/dszc

Perseverance is not a long race; it is many short races, one after another.

—Walter Elliott

In the state of Texas, as in many other states, there is a rigorous certification examination that potential administrators must pass before they are eligible for certification. In Texas this test is called the TExES (Texas Examination of Educator Standards). There is tremendous pressure on future leaders to pass this test. Without it, they cannot become certified. There is also tremendous pressure on preparation programs for their students to do well because their programs are judged based on their pass-fail rates. Potential test takers from both inside and outside the state are looking for tools to help them achieve their goal of certification and reaching the principalship. This book describes how to become the world's best principal through awesome leadership preparation.

Universities and alternative preparation programs are working hard to address both the knowledge and the philosophical bases on which TExES is framed. The new 268 TExES Exam for principals is built on a foundation of eleven competencies within six domains. Its creators assume that test takers have received knowledge and research preparation through their educational providers. This book supplies needed supplemental resources for the knowledge base, but it is not intended to substitute for a quality master's degree. It focuses, however, on the philosophy necessary to think like a learner-centered principal. Many students find it difficult to make the transition from thinking like a teacher to thinking, reflecting, reacting, and responding like a principal. All the knowledge in the world is useless if a test taker cannot think in the way the test was developed. *Passing the Principal as Instructional Leader TExES Exam: Keys to Certification and School Leadership, Third Edition* addresses this philosophy as well as the skills that principals must have within each of the six domains and eleven competencies. It provides test-taking tips for before, during, and after the exam. Specific attention is given to in-state and out-of-state test takers. The volume also provides practice test questions grouped into decision sets within a mini test. Each competency chapter concludes with additional resources that are helpful to students as they develop the knowledge and philosophical bases necessary to pass the test and pursue careers as lifelong learners.

Finally, this third edition is written in an informal, first-person voice. There are real-life stories and applications integrated into each competency to help the reader tie concepts to reality. It is absolutely necessary that test takers apply their knowledge and skills to the test—as well as to life in general. In a friendly, supportive manner, *Passing the Principal as Instructional Leader TExES Exam* helps test takers and others interested in learner-centered leadership integrate TExES competencies and domains into real-world application. The original 2002 edition, as well as the second edition, became an instant Corwin best seller and remains as such to this day. It is used by universities and alternative preparation programs, as well as individual students, across the state. This third edition continues to be based on domains and competencies provided through Texas law and developed by the Texas State Board for Educator Certification (SBEC) and the success of the two previous editions. It is written based on the years of experience Wilmore has as a teacher, counselor, principal, professor, and school board member and providing popular, successful, and inspiring TExES preparation seminars at universities, webinars, regional service centers, and other training sites around the state. In addition, this updated version also includes updates to the TExES exam and additional test-taking strategies developed since the original printing.

Let's see how.

BASIC CONCEPTS

The principal TExES is divided into six domains with eleven competencies. These domains are as follows:

- School Culture
- Leading Learning
- Human Capital
- Executive Leadership
- Strategic Operations
- Ethics, Equity, and Diversity

Questions on the test are designed to address specific competencies. They are not evenly divided, but every competency is addressed. The number of competencies per domain are shown in Figure 1.1.

FIGURE 1.1   Domains and Competencies

DOMAIN	# OF COMPETENCIES
DOMAIN I: School Culture	2
DOMAIN II: Leading Learning	2
DOMAIN III: Human Capital	2
DOMAIN IV: Executive Leadership	2
DOMAIN V: Strategic Operations	2
DOMAIN VI: Ethics, Equity, and Diversity	1

There is no absolute number of questions per competency or domain. My goal is for *all* my students to get *all* the questions correct, regardless of which domain or competency a question comes from. Nonetheless, a student does not have to score 100% to pass the test. For many students, simply realizing they do not have to earn a perfect score on the test helps take off some of the pressure. This is a benefit because half the battle of passing this test is your mindset. In other words, you must know that you can, and will, succeed. It is my intention for everyone reading this book to win the mind game. You should walk in to take the test feeling cool, calm, collected, confident—and even downright cocky; you should walk out feeling the same. This mental attitude is necessary to lower your level of stress. When your stress level goes up, your productivity goes down (see Figure 1.2). We want your stress level down and your productivity to be way up. Therefore, you should be cool, calm, collected,

FIGURE 1.2   When Stress Goes Up, Productivity Goes Down

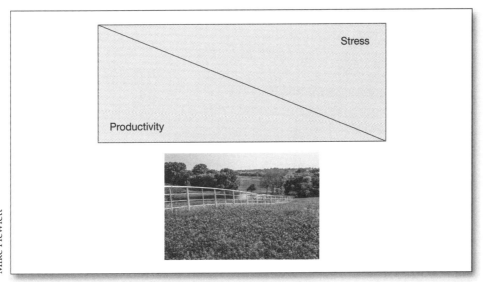

Mike Hewlett

confident, and downright cocky throughout both your preparation and the test-taking experience.

Many people place great emphasis on discerning exactly which competency each question addresses. Although I discuss this strategy, it does not receive undue attention. Remember, if our goal is to get every question correct, why do we care from which competency the question came? We do not; we want to get all the questions right. Nonetheless, upon becoming thoroughly familiar with each of the competencies, as you will by reading Chapters 5 through 15, you will recognize key words and concepts that will guide your selection of the appropriate answers to get all the questions right—or at least enough questions right to pass.

In addition, there is significant overlap of key themes within the competencies. Since the test is largely a timed mind game, why would you want to get stressed out, with the clock ticking, by worrying if a question is addressing competency 001 or 003? Who cares? The important thing is to understand, integrate, and live the competencies. Make them your "school administrator's bible." Beginning this minute, let your walk match your talk in modeling these competencies in your daily life. Then on the day of the test, walk in there and ace TExES because you are already "walking the talk!"

LEADERSHIP: A SKILL OR AN ART?

There has been, and likely always will be, considerable discussion of whether good leadership is a skill that can be studied or an art that is practiced as diligently as master painters practice their own art form, working hard to produce a masterpiece. For years, researchers such as Kent Peterson, Lee Bolman, and Terrence Deal have presented a view of school leadership that blends concepts of skill and art. Indeed, leadership is a blend of art and skill. Skills are absolutely necessary for good leadership, but they must be practiced and nurtured into the nuances of an art. Never forget that leadership is a talent. Develop it. Nurture it in yourself and in others. Your school, as well as you personally and others whom your leadership affects, will benefit.

Think of leadership as a really good jazz band. As the musicians practice before a performance, they individually sound like a whole lot of noise. They are all doing their own thing, warming up, and getting ready for the concert. But once the performance begins, everything comes together. The musicians play as a team. They are people who have worked hard, practiced together, and who have the common goal of producing really beautiful music. Because they have done those things, the concert begins, and their skills turn into an art as they blend together, bending and flowing with the crescendos and decrescendos, the tempo, and the dynamics of the music to produce something truly beautiful.

Our schools deserve leaders who are orchestrating a wonderful jazz band. As long as everyone in the school is doing their own thing, independent of each other, it is just noise. Although some progress may be made, everyone's skills are acting independently. They are not making beautiful music. But with a great leader—a learner-centered leader with passion, vision, and purpose—the school of musicians can win a Grammy. Every child in every school deserves to be a part of that jazz band, the jazz band that produces artful music, not noise. Every child deserves to be a part of a learning team. Every child deserves to be a part of a school whose staff members are focused on their success in every facet of their lives. Every child deserves the chance to come away a winner.

For too many students today, there is little hope for the future. It is my goal that you become the leader of your school's jazz band. You will be the leader who does what is right instead of what is easy or bureaucratic. You will be the principal who facilitates your school in developing a common vision and a solid purpose built on identified common values. You will be the one to change the world . . . or at least your campus. You will become an awesome principal, or I will come back and haunt you.

But first, you must pass the TExES. Are you ready to get started?

GETTING STARTED

Section II of this book includes Chapters 5 through 15. Chapter 2, "Standing on the Promises," provides the global overview of how you will achieve your goal of passing this test. It is merely a gatekeeper designed to see that you have a specific learner-centered philosophy of school leadership as portrayed in the domains and competencies. It requires entry-level administrative skills and expectations, and it is a passable test. You *will* pass this test.

I teach school leadership. I also teach TExES preparation seminars and webinars all over the state. It brings me great joy when students from any of them contact me to let me know they passed the test. I get really excited! After all, that means there is one more human out there ready to join my journey toward improving the world. And when you pass, you can send me chocolate (plain Hershey bars, please), roses (I prefer pink), or ice cream (Blue Bell, of course). Chapters 5 through 15 give detailed attention to each of the eleven learner-centered competencies. If you have never even heard of them up to this point, that is all right. By the time I get through with you, you will be living and breathing them. If not, you are in a coma. Check with your doctor. It is time to wake up to get ready for this test. You are going to know those competencies inside out. You will be reciting them to your families and friends. If you do not have family or friends, I strongly suggest finding some. They will be a great support system—and they'll be there to celebrate when you pass the test!

Section III addresses the integration and application of all you have learned in Section II. You will become skilled at how to analyze data, learn specific test-taking strategies, create your own Personal Success Plan, and then tie it all together in Section IV, "That's What It's All About." By the time you walk in to take the TExES exam, you will be so well prepared that all you will want to do is go in and pass it so you can go forward to improve the world and eat more chocolate. My goal is to help you pass the test so you can help change the world one school at a time. This test is just a nuisance to get in your way until then. So let's get rid of the nuisance by passing the test the first time.

Are you ready? Let's go!

CHAPTER 2
Updates to Test Structure: 068 to 268

If we knew what we were doing, it wouldn't be called research.

—**Albert Einstein**

There have been previous updates to the Principal TExES Exam (068) that have been barely noticeable. That is not true with the update from 068 to 268. They are totally different tests. Whereas 068 was strictly a multiple-choice test, albeit some of the questions being "multiple-multiples," 268 goes way beyond multiple-choice questions. While the multiple-choice questions are still there, additional types of questions have been added. Those are discussed here.

When 068 was first introduced in 2002, the role of the principal was seen as the building *Manager*. Today, in 268, the principal is seen as the *Instructional Leader*. At that time the Professional Development and Assessment System (PDAS) was used for summative teacher evaluation. Today the T-TESS is used for continual assessment via coaching. In 2002, K–12 students were taking the Texas Assessment of Academic Skills (TAAS) test. Now they are taking the STAAR test. Finally, before campuses were rated as Exemplary, Recognized, or Acceptable. Now, they are actually scored on an A to F basis. Obviously, a lot has changed, which has led to the development and implementation of 268. It has been a transition that started with the new principal standards in 2016 to the new 268 exam in 2018.

The new test will continue to be a 5-hour test consisting of 100 "selected response" (SR) questions and four "constructed response" (CR) items, which are discussed shortly. There *will* be some items on the test that do not actually count toward your score. You just won't know which ones they are. All the questions are built around a new framework consisting of six domains, eleven competencies, and with new descriptors for each. The most significant descriptors are called Priority Descriptors and are noted by being printed in bold print. In this book, I refer to them the same way: in bold print. This book addresses all the descriptors, whether they are Priority Descriptors or not, because you need to know and understand them all to be able to apply them as demonstrated by selecting the correct answers to the questions.

The eleven competencies are grouped around specific "pillars." These pillars are

1. Communication With Stakeholders

2. Curriculum Alignment

3. Diversity and Equity

4. Data-Driven Instruction

5. Hiring, Selection, and Retention

6. Observation and Feedback

7. Professional Development

8. School Vision and Culture

9. Strategic Problem Solving

Discussion of each pillar is woven throughout this book.

The new domains, competencies, and descriptors, with the pillars interwoven, are not a rehash of the 068 three domains and nine competencies, but a brand-new framework. Will there be some similarities? Of course. We still want all students to be successful as well as wanting to serve all our students equitably. But the domains and competencies are different, the test structures can be different, you will need to utilize correct writing skills, and you will have to apply even greater higher-order thinking skills to select the right responses.

Items are weighted this time with a likely weighting of 60% SRs and 40% CRs. Some SR and CR items will contain a video stimulus for you to respond to. This is also a major change from 068.

The Selected Response item domains are

• School Culture

• Leading Learning

• Human Capitol

• Executive Leadership

• Strategic Operations

• Ethics, Equity, and Diversity

Constructed Responses (CR) are tested from Domains I, II, and III. These are

- School Culture

- Leading Learning

- Human Capital

The SR multiple-choice questions are similar to the ones in 068. The distinction comes with the CR questions, which are open ended and require you to utilize both your higher-level thinking skills and your writing skills. They are the reason for the increase in cost of 268 over 068, and 068 could be graded completely by a computer, and you could receive your results quickly. Due to the CR questions in 268, that is not possible. Trained raters must read and score your CR responses individually. The hand grading of the CR responses takes much more time and human effort than computer grading, thus, the increase in price. They will apply rubrics per question as shown in the *Preparation Manual: A Candidate and Program Planning Guide, Principal as Instructional Leader* (268) (http://cms.texes-ets.org/files/9115/3297/0895/TX_268_principal_prep_manual.pdf). It shows examples of types of questions you could be asked in a CR situation with proposed scoring rubrics. It is an excellent resource, one you definitely should download and utilize. However, it does not teach you the domains and competencies. This book does that. Therefore, you need both.

All in all, the purpose of both 068 and 268 is the same: to ensure beginning principals have the knowledge and skills to truly be an Instructional Leader and to run a productive campus their first year. By clearly understanding and being able to answer questions coherently regarding the six domains and eleven competencies, you are proving exactly that. By studying this book, you are off in the right direction to *ace* this test!

CHAPTER 3
Principal Assessment of School Leadership (PASL)

iStock/dszc

The best index to a person's character is how they treat people who can't do them any good.

—**Abigail Van Buren**

WHAT'S IT ALL ABOUT, ALPHIE?

The purpose of this book is to prepare you for passing the 268 *Principal as Instructional Leader* TExES Exam, not the Principal Assessment of School Leadership (PASL). However, the PASL will soon be compulsory, so it is in your best interest to at least know what it is all about.

In large part, the PASL is conducted through your internship or practicum. In Texas, it is aligned with the Texas Principal Certificate Standards. (See Addendum C.) The Principal TExES Exam is aligned with these same standards. There is information regarding preparation materials at https://www.ets.org/ppa/test-takers/school-leaders/prepare/. This link is also a good overview of the entire PASL process, so do check it out. Basically, it continues the theme of focusing on the students and their success.

Scores per tasks are determined by rubrics. A sample rubric for Task 2 is provided at https://www.ets.org/s/ppa/pdf/ppat-task-2-rubric.pdf.

The PASL is only administered twice a year. In both instances, you will submit your work/evidence online. Due to the hand grading, it will take 3 to 4 weeks to get your scores. Like the TExES Exam, passing the PASL is mandatory before you can apply for principal certification.

The basic PASL framework consists of three tasks, which evidence your competence in that specific area:

- **Task 1:** Problem Solving in the Field, https://www.ets.org/s/ppa/pdf/pasl-task-1-overview.pdf

- **Task 2:** Supporting Continuous Professional Development, https://www.ets.org/s/ppa/pdf/pasl-task-2-overview.pdf

- **Task 3:** Creating a Collaborative Culture, https://www.ets.org/s/ppa/pdf/pasl-task-3-overview.pdf

Ancillary Materials to help you with PASL are available at https://www.ets.org/ppa/test-takers/school-leaders/build-submit/ancillary-materials.

Frequently Asked Questions are available at https://www.ets.org/ppa/test-takers/school-leaders/faq/.

However, right now PASL is not your top priority. Passing the TExES Exam is your top priority. This quick chapter is simply to give you an overview of the PASL process and to provide you with links to where you can find important additional information on your own. But do not dwell on this too much until after you pass your TExES Exam. It is the Big Dog on Campus.

SECTION II

Philosophy

The Theoretical Framework

CHAPTER 4
Standing on the Promises

iStock/dszc

Vision without execution is hallucination.

—Thomas Edison

GLOBAL OVERVIEW OF TExES DOMAINS

It is helpful to understand "the big picture" of the theoretical framework—that is, the competencies and domains—on which the new TExES (268) is built before we get into the details of the competencies. As introduced in Chapter 1, the eleven competencies are placed into six domains. These are:

1. School Culture
2. Leading Learning
3. Human Capital
4. Executive Leadership
5. Strategic Operations
6. Ethics, Equity, and Diversity

There is significant overlap in the integration of the individual competencies because a principalship is not a segmented, compartmentalized job. Daily roles and tasks overlap. While fighting the fires of a normal school day, does the average principal stop to ask, "Gee, I wonder if I should respond through Competency 002 or 006?" Definitely not! This is why you should know the competencies inside and out and internalize their concepts so that you can respond reflectively and instinctively. It is not necessary to memorize the competencies. It is necessary to truly *understand* what they mean. What are the test framers trying to tell you? What they are trying to tell you is what you should look for in potential responses. Pick answers aligned with their philosophy. Give them answers they want to hear. You will know that by fastidiously studying this book.

Before getting into the detailed analysis of the competencies within Chapters 5 through 15, let us discuss specific components in format and the theoretical framework of the domains.

KEY CONCEPTS

I provide three key concepts per domain to help you identify and keep them straight—both as you prepare for the test and afterward as you grow as a principal. These key words capture the basic essence of what each domain is about. They will help you focus as you dig deeper into the concepts they represent in the competencies. During the test, the concepts they represent serve as clues to identifying the right answers.

PRIORITY DESCRIPTORS

Something new has been added to the way the descriptors under each competency are displayed. Under each competency, some of the descriptors are in bold print. But not all of them. It is this way for all eleven competencies. This is not an error.

The reason some of the descriptors are bolded is they are the ones the test makers deem the most important for that competency. Since they are considered the most important, there is a good chance you will see more questions from those descriptors than from the descriptors that are not bolded. This is a hint to you. Ensure that you understand all the descriptors, but be especially sure you understand the Priority Descriptors.

In each competency chapter (5–15), I bold the Priority Descriptors just like they do. But at the end of each of these chapters I do a summary of the Priority Descriptors for that competency in one place so you can find them quickly. Since you know the Priority Descriptors are their favorites, make sure you understand them and are prepared to answer questions based on their content and philosophy.

THE IDEAL PRINCIPAL

For just a few minutes, stop and close your eyes. Visualize in your mind an ideal principal whom you know, or with whom you have worked. If you cannot think of an ideal principal, make one up. Perhaps your person will be a combination of the skills or talents of several different principals who you know or wish you knew. Think about all the things this real or imaginary person does or could do. What makes her or him great? What attributes or characteristics does this principal have? What makes the person better than the average principal? What makes this principal outstanding? Take a few minutes to really think about this. *Do not blow off this exercise!*

After you open your eyes, write on a piece of paper the adjectives or other words you used to describe this ideal principal in your mind. Take several minutes to do this. At first, obvious characteristics will come to your mind. Fine. Write them down.

When you think you have thought of them all, dig a little deeper. Come up with some more. It is in this deep reflection that you will get to the heart of the traits of the ideal principal. List twenty to thirty. You can do it! Dig deep, and come up with some more really good ones. Write them down. From now till eternity, but particularly the day you take the test, you are that principal. You are ideal. Think, breathe, and eat ideal. Be the ideal principal as you pick the ideal responses. Remember, this test is not based on reality. The test designers know you know what reality looks like. They want to know if you know what ideal looks like. The questions are designed to see if you know that. After all, if you don't know what ideal looks like, how are you going to lead a campus toward it? As shown in Figure 4.1, ideal principals are effective principals because they keep their focus on the needs of the students.

FIGURE 4.1   The Ideal Principal Will Focus on the Needs of the Students

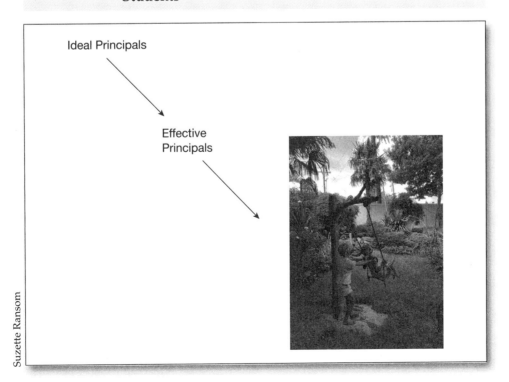

Ideal Principals

Effective Principals

Suzette Ransom

If possible, prepare for the test with a friend. Study and discuss this book together. Do this exercise together. Then compare your results. Your results will multiply as you collaborate. You will likely have identified many common characteristics, and that's fine. Great principals *do* have many things in common. However, you and your friend may also have come up with different characteristics. Are they things you can agree on? Are they things you both agree constitute this new "mega-ideal principal"? Come up with a master list of characteristics of the ideal principal. Discuss them together. Keep this composite to review periodically before the test. Why did you select these traits and not others? Elaborate on your thought process. This is what becoming a reflective practitioner is all about. This exercise is worth true effort, and it will help you pass the test.

Once you have developed your ideal principal, think about that principal and no other for the rest of your life. Think about that person as you study the domains and competencies. Think about the ideal principal as you select responses to the practice decision set questions at the end of this book. Above all, think only about the ideal principal on the day you take TExES. Do not think, "That's unreasonable," or "That response isn't practical." Forget reasonable and practical! Think ideal! You can be reasonable and practical when you are picking out a new car. On test day, think *ideal principal!* Think, "Dr. Wilmore says, 'Forget reasonable and practical. Think ideal!'" As shown in Figure 4.1, there are enough reasonable and practical principals out there who have totally lost sight of the vision and purpose of the school. Think ideal to change the world—one student and school at a time. Besides, what you learn from this book will haunt you if you ever turn into a bureaucrat.

PRETEND

Remember when you were a child and played pretend games? It was fun to pretend to be an astronaut or President of the United States. (You're never too old to play make-believe!) Well, let's play the pretend game again. Let's say that you are not into this whole "ideal principal" concept. Let's say that thinking "ideal" is just too far-fetched and would never work in the real world. Let's say that you cannot think of a single good reason to hold the ideal principal up as a standard for making TExES exam answer choices.

Pretend you believe you can become an ideal principal and really affect your school. Imagine how you would feel if this were so. Savor that feeling and work toward it forever. There is no law that says you have to believe in any of the traits of the ideal principal. Maybe your goal in life is to be a bureaucrat. If this is true, I have two suggestions:

1. On the day of the test, pretend like crazy! You may not buy the philosophy of the ideal principal, but I can guarantee one thing. The developers of this test do, and they hold all the cards. Therefore, if you want to pass this test, pretend like crazy.

2. What if you can't do it? You simply do not buy one word of this "ideal principal" concept. You really do want to become a bureaucrat. You have a burning desire to sit in the principal's office listening to Mozart, doing as little as possible, and never actually become invested in the lives of others. Nonetheless, you'd like to look important while you do nothing. Here's my suggestion. Put away this book. It will do nothing for you except raise your blood pressure.

You've learned the way you're supposed to think to pass this test and change the world, and you've learned to pretend on test day—that is, if you have difficulty with the concept of the ideal principal. Now it's time to get started with the six domains.

Important Recurring Themes and Concepts: The Sherrys

It can be overwhelming to look at the entire Principal TExES preparation manual and see all those pages of domains, competencies, and practice decision sets. However, it is not nearly as daunting as it may seem. The test developers actually have some favorite concepts and use them repeatedly. They simply spin them different directions within each of the six domains. However, if you spot a Sherry, or a Sherry synonym, take it as a strong hint! Remember, if Mama had liked a name better than Sherry, she would have named the baby that name. Similarly, if you see Sherrys in a response, give it an extra hard look because it is probably the answer.

Think of it this way. If a new set of parents name their baby "Sherry" and "Sherry" is not a family name, we can assume they must like the name Sherry. The same is true with this TExES exam. There are themes and concepts that the domains and competencies use over and over. We call them our Sherrys. Just as new parents must like a name or they would not have picked it, the same is true for us. Once we identify the Sherrys when we see them in answer options, we realize they are there for a reason. The test developers like them. They are the test Sherrys. Pick and use them accordingly. A sampling of Sherrys appears in Figure 4.2, Important Recurring Themes and Concepts: The "Sherry" List. Watch for the Sherrys in Chapters 5 through 15, see if you can identify more, and be particularly vigilant to watch for them as you take the actual examination.

THE SIX DOMAINS

Domain I: School Culture

Key Concepts: Culture, Vision, and School and Community Leadership

Domain I is all about *school culture*. I love this domain. It is my personal favorite. It likely will not take you long to figure out why.

FIGURE 4.2   Important Recurring Themes and Concepts:
The "Sherry" List

• All	• Professional development
• Alignment	• Enhancing everything: How can I make it better?
• Collaborate	• Ongoing, continuous assessment
• Data-based decisions	• Multiple and diverse forms of assessment and measurement
• The 1–2–3–4 Plan	• High expectations
• Develop—create—design	• Facilitate
• Articulate—communicate—market	• Student advocate
• Implement—put into action	• Student needs
• Evaluate—assess	• Participatory leadership and management
• Culture	
• Climate	
• Vision	
• Lifelong learning	

In a nutshell, school culture leadership concentrates on all the things a principal should do to develop and nurture a culture, climate, and vision of the school whose staff members are supportive of all stakeholders and help them succeed. Who is a stakeholder? Everyone. Absolutely no one is left out. Stakeholders go hand-in-hand with another key TExES term and concept: the *learning community* or *school community*. The idea is to get everyone, all stakeholders, possible involved in identifying common values, developing a shared purpose and vision of the school, and developing goals and strategies to achieve them. The school community consists of teachers, counselors, paraprofessionals, auxiliary personnel, parents, community members, businesses, churches, and everyone else interested in the school. The more people you can get involved, the better. People support what they help build. Our schools need all the help and support they can get. This theoretical framework is shown in Figure 4.3 by all eleven competencies upon which you will be tested being focused on student success.

You may ask, "What if my school is simply awful? What if it is located in a part of town where no one wants to go? It is dangerous. The idea of getting parents or anyone else involved is pretty far-fetched." Fine. Think far-fetched. Remember, we are focused on the ideal principal. The ideal principal learned at the feet of Winston Churchill. During the bleakest moments of World War II, Churchill was known for telling the English that their nation would never, never give up. England never did

FIGURE 4.3   The Eleven Domain Competencies Focus on Student Success

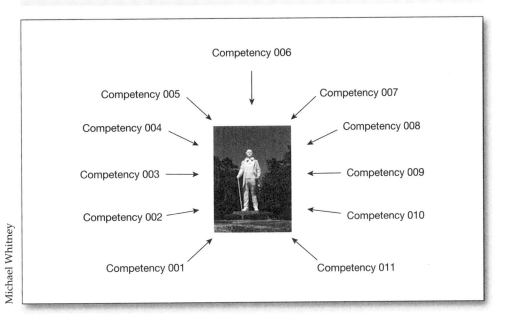

Michael Whitney

give up. Eventually, the Allies won the war, preserving freedom and democracy for the next generation. It did not happen by taking the easy road or rolling over and playing dead. It happened through hard work, perseverance, and collaboration with other countries.

The same is true within Domain I. The ideal principal will never give up. It doesn't matter how bleak the circumstances; ideal principals pick themselves up, dust themselves off, and start all over again. They ask themselves, "How can I do this better next time?" Why do they ask themselves that? Because there is *always* a next time. Therefore, we need to make every unsuccessful venture a learning opportunity. Either we grow and learn from our mistakes or we keep making the same ones over and over. That's called settling for the status quo.

The ideal principal abhors the status quo. The ideal principal is always striving to make every single thing better. Making every single thing better is how we move toward ideal.

It takes intense resiliency to be a great school principal. Anyone can be a lackluster, status quo principal. Who on Earth needs more of those? Certainly not us! We are Domain I principals, intent on facilitating collaboration for a better tomorrow. It's a vision thing. Never give up. Never.

Can you see why this domain is my favorite?

Domain II: Leading Learning

Key Concepts: Instructional Leadership, Teaching, and Learning

Domain II is the "meat and potatoes" of the principalship. It is what makes us different from chief executive officers or managers of any other organization. We are here to lead schools, not shoe stores. What are we selling? Curriculum and instruction. How do we do that? Through more relevant staff development. Why is this important? To improve student achievement.

Notice, I did not say simply *teacher* staff development. That would be limiting. As lifelong learners we believe in developing and nurturing *all* people—that includes *all* stakeholders at the school and beyond. We do not want to limit anything or anyone. Motivational speaker Les Brown says to reach for the moon. Even if you do not reach it, you will land among the stars. Awesome principals want to nurture and develop everyone. They reach for the moon and settle for the stars only if they have to. However, landing among the stars sure beats being in the pits with low student achievement.

Always dream big. I tell my students that if they do not remember one other thing that I teach them, to remember to dream big dreams. I even have it on my voice mail. You would be surprised how many people leave messages commenting about what a surprise it is to hear anyone encouraging them to "dream big." I always wonder, isn't dreaming big what universities are all about?

In fact, isn't that what all schools are for? Domain II is about improving instruction, teacher effectiveness, and producing enhanced achievement for the benefit of all students. It's about finding ways to nurture and develop stakeholders so they can be the arms and legs for improved curriculum and instruction and to meet the developmental needs of all students.

This would be a good time to introduce the Texas Assessment of Knowledge and Skills (TAKS) and the State of Texas Assessments of Academic Readiness, commonly called STAAR.

STAAR, and TAKS before it, begin in the third grade and continue through Grade 8. It was originally given primarily in reading, math, and writing with secondary schools also reporting End-of-Course (EOC) test results. Subsequently, tests in both science and social studies were added. Some subjects, such as writing, science, and social studies, are not given in every grade; thus, there will not be any scores reported for the grades in which they are not given. Currently, STAAR is not given on the secondary level. Secondary EOC exams are currently given in 12 areas. These are English I, English II, English III, Algebra I, Algebra II, Geography, World Geography, World History, U.S. History, Biology, Chemistry, and Physics. Test results are reported in the first section of the Texas Academic Performance Report (TAPR) (Addendum B) because all testing information is at the front regardless if it is elementary or secondary.

For out-of-state test takers, STAAR and the EOCs are really big tests in Texas. Students begin taking it in the third grade. They keep taking it until they pass the high school version. If students do not pass the high school TAKS, they do not graduate, period. It doesn't matter if they make straight As. It doesn't matter how many honors or advanced placement classes they have taken. It doesn't matter if they have a wonderful scholarship waiting for them. They must pass that test. Students who fail STAAR in the early grades are identified as *at risk*. Plans are made to remediate them so they will pass the following year, to help get them on track for the high school exam. The public schools of Texas are under intense pressure for students to do well on both STAAR and the EOCs. The state accountability system is directly linked to student success or failure on them. The TExES refers to TAKS, because it was around so long, and now STAAR and EOCs many times. It is not the purpose of this book to address whether this high-stakes testing is a good thing or a bad thing. It doesn't matter—it's the law. And if it's the law, then it's the hand we're dealt. And if it's the hand we're playing, you can guess what we must do. *Win!*

If we think of state exams as important games that we intend to win, we must become coaches and produce game plans and strategies to make sure we do. How many coaches do you know who say, "Well, guys, it's Friday night in Texas. Half the town will be out there waiting to see you play. They don't really care if you win or lose. They just want to see you looking good in those great uniforms." Right. In *Texas?* I don't think so. In Texas, teams are expected to win. If they do not, serious things can happen. It is downright un-Texan!

Domain II is about winning. Think "instruction, teacher effectiveness, and student achievement." They are our tools for winning. They are our game plan. They are the "meat and potatoes" of who we are and why we are here. To create a better world, we must have an educated society. Meat and potatoes. Instruction, teacher effectiveness, and student achievement. Domain II. Think winning!

Domain III: Human Capital

Key Concepts: Professional Development,
HR Management, and Personnel and Self-Appraisal

Domain III takes a different direction from Domains I and II. It is all about professional development, reflection, and growth for all. It is absolutely necessary that principals are committed and passionate about the campus vision and that they do everything possible to augment appropriate curriculum and instruction. Still, if principals cannot appropriately focus and lead regarding professional development, reflection, and growth for all stakeholders, ultimately they will not be successful.

No one, no matter how experienced, knows everything. They may think they know everything, but they don't. We ALL need professional development to grow and not become stagnant. The best way to determine the individual professional development needs for all stakeholders is to look at the students. If a certain teacher's class is scoring low in estimation skills, then that tells us that teacher needs help teaching estimation skills. Ditto for a different teacher whose students may be scoring poorly in reading comprehension skills. That is where their professional development should be steered. The general rule is to determine where teachers need help, look at the scores of their students. The students' lowest areas should be the top priorities for these teachers.

Likewise with reflection. Reflection is an incredibly important tool when used appropriately. We all should set aside time to look at our professional practice. We must objectively and genuinely examine our practice to determine for ourselves where we need to focus at least some of our professional development. This is the way we grow rather than teaching exactly the same way we did 10 years ago. Society has changed. Students and their homes have changed. Why should our practice stay the same? We must constantly evaluate what we are doing and continuously ask ourselves, "How can I do this better?" This will maximize teacher effectiveness and encourage greater student growth.

Domain IV: Executive Leadership

Key Concepts: Communication, Organizational Management, and Improving Student Outcomes

Domain IV focuses on both internal and external communication with others, building relationships among diverse people and populations, and improving student outcomes. To reach all stakeholders we must have both internal (inside the school) communication as well as external (outside the school) communication. It is imperative that the right hand knows what and why the other is doing something. Like the old saying says, "We must be on the same page of the hymnal" or we will have a mess. Likewise, ideal principals work hard at creating positive relationships inside and outside the school. I promise you that no matter how good a principal you are, someday something ridiculous will happen and you will be left holding the bag. At this point your credibility will be tested inside the school and in the community. If you have built a firm foundation through solid relationships, those relationships will come back to stand by your side and help you and/or your campus through the dark times.

The opposite is also true, but we won't go there. It is obvious.

Student outcomes are sisters with student achievement. They consist of the individual goals that each student has met. The ones they have mastered, or not mastered, are their outcomes. Some students will master all their goals, some may not master any, and even more may be a mixture of mastering some, but not all their goals. Our job is to do everything in our power to create a learning environment, utilize appropriate instructional strategies, and providing relevant professional development with a goal of 100% mastery. You may not think that is realistic. But remember, on this test you are to forget reality and think ideal. In an ideal school all the teachers would be individualizing instruction, and all the students would be mastering all their objectives.

It is the *ideal* way, and on this test, everything is ideal.

Domain V: Strategic Operations

Key Concepts: Goals, Alignment, and Resource Allocation

All campuses will, or should, have goals as a part of their Campus Improvement Plan. These goals should be developed by multiple stakeholders and based on the needs of the students. How do we know the needs of the students?

We look at test scores, find the lowest areas, and focus on those. You may say, "My campus is low on everything." Obviously, you cannot significantly address everything as a specific goal in one school year. Therefore, pick three to five of the most pressing issues and target them as your goals.

Once your goals are identified, what are you going to do to address and meet them? In other words, what exactly are you going to do to move your campus from where it is to where you want it to be as stated in your goal? These are the strategies that the campus with all its stakeholders are going to utilize to master the goal. On that subject, goals without accountability (deadlines, percentage of improvement, etc.) are not goals. They are dreams. Dr. John Hoyle of Texas A&M was my professor, then mentor and friend. When he passed away, I felt like someone had kicked me *hard* in the stomach. John was a truly idealistic professor and a great human being. He used to say, "Goals without deadlines are only dreams." Think about that. If we say we want to improve reading comprehension scores, but do not say by what percentage or by what point in time, do we really have a measurable goal? Of course not. We only have a dream. Therefore, always make your goals measurable and state by what point in time you expect to achieve them. That's called accountability.

To maximize the impact of your goals and strategies, your campus needs to provide a safe and nurturing learning environment where students feel free to learn and to make mistakes or ask for extra help as necessary. People often underestimate the value of a safe and effective learning environment. But consider it this way. Say you went into a department store you had never been in. You wanted a new pair of boots, but you were totally clueless where to look in this massive store. There were sales people all around, but not one of them came up to see if they could help you.

How would you feel? Would that be a nurturing environment for a customer?

Nope.

But if the salespeople saw you and one came directly to you with a smile and asked whether they could help you, then that would be a good, nurturing environment.

It is the same way at schools. We must make visitors feel welcome, as well as providing that "home away from home" for the students. That's a nurturing learning environment.

Last is the huge issue of school safety. Even since the last edition of this book, school violence has come more and more to the forefront. Texas law mandates every campus and district have a Crisis Management Plan. They do not prescribe what must actually be in it, but it should cover just about anything that could happen that impacts school safety. It also requires that once you have a Crisis Management Plan, you practice it. A monthly fire drill, while a start, is not enough to fulfill this requirement. Different variations of the Crisis Management Plan should be practiced. Exterior doors should be locked. You should, at a minimum, have access to Campus Security. Let the Site-Based Team work on helping develop this as you serve as the facilitator. Why? Because people support what they help create.

Domain VI: Ethics, Equity, and Diversity

Key Concepts: Ethics, Equity, and Diversity

Domain VI is our shortest domain, but that does not mean it is any less important than the other five. We must all be ethical whether we are alone or with students, parents, or any member of the school community. We all must be advocates for the needs of all students, standing up for those who need it the most and do not have anyone else to stand up for them. You may be thinking this sounds really personal. Guess what. It *is*. But it is necessary to stand up for the two groups in our society that are the most vulnerable: our very young and our elderly. How we treat these two groups says a lot about who we are as a people, as a school, and as a nation. We are putting our actions where our mouths are. Anyone can sing a pretty song. But we are not looking for pretty songs. We are looking for *action*! Take a chance. Be proactive by being an advocate for all students!

The ideal principal never gives up. The ideal principal works constantly, without letting up, to maintain a safe and effective learning environment for all students. Anything less is simply going through the motions.

You have now been introduced to the global overview of the six learner-centered domains. The next eleven chapters delve into the specificity of the eleven competencies that fall within these six domains. From the beginning you will know that if a competency—or a test question—has something to do with culture, vision, or stakeholders, it is likely a Domain I question. You should look for a test response that also directly relates to the same issue. The same is true for the other five domains. To keep your domains straight, remember your key concepts.

Remember as well that sometimes the TExES provides what seems to be an excellent answer choice but that doesn't answer the question to which it refers. If you are nervous and see an answer choice that says, "George Washington was the first President of the United States," you may think, "That's right!" But remember, the question had nothing to do with George Washington. A nervous mind can play tricks on you, so beware! Make sure you pick the answer that is aligned with this specific question. On the provided paper, write down important words in the prompt and the question to keep you focused on exactly what is asked. If the test gives you a wonderful selection choice, but it doesn't apply to the question and isn't in line with the appropriate domain, forget it. It may be beautiful, but it isn't the right answer to the question. Now let's take a look at those eleven competencies. The next eleven chapters go into detail on each of them.

Now let's get started with Domain I, Competency 001!

CHAPTER 5
Learner-Centered Leadership and Campus Culture

iStock/dszc

The key to success is not to prioritize your schedule, but to schedule your priorities.

—Stephen Covey

Domain I: School Culture

Domain Key Concepts:
Culture, Vision, and Stakeholders

Competency 001

The beginning principal knows how to establish and implement a shared vision and culture of high expectations for all stakeholders (students, staff, parents, and community).

This competency is loaded with Sherrys. Pay attention to them. A shared vision is one of the most important issues a principal can establish and implement. Without it everyone is doing their own thing, maybe, or maybe not, setting classroom goals that may, or may not, be aligned to any campus goals that may, or may not, exist! The same is true of a culture that has high expectations of learning for everyone. This includes the students, staff, parents, and the community. Combined these constitute the school's stakeholders.

THE PRINCIPAL KNOWS HOW TO . . .

A. *Creates a positive, collaborative, and collegial campus culture that sets high expectations and facilitates the implementation and achievement of campus initiatives and goals.*

Descriptor A is almost a restatement of competency 001 itself only using different words. It is the principal's responsibility to create, or develop, a positive, collaborative, and collegial school culture that sets high expectations and facilitates (or assists in making happen) the implementation and achievement of campus initiatives (e.g., programs, strategies, etc.) and goals. These goals must, of course, be collaboratively developed for the betterment of the school and aligned with student needs.

FIGURE 5.1   All Campus, Department, and Grade-Level Goals Should Be Student Focused

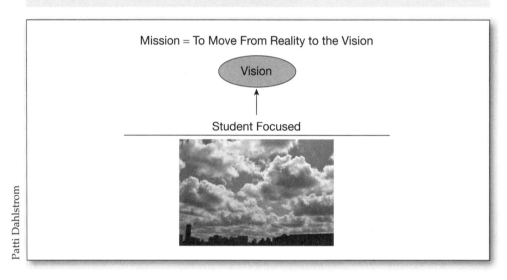

B. *Uses emerging issues, recent research, knowledge of systems (e.g., school improvement process, strategic planning, etc.) and various types of data (e.g., demographic, perceptive, student learning, and processes) to collaboratively develop a shared campus vision and a plan for implementing the vision.*

FIGURE 5.2   Visons and Goal Setting Alignment—All Goals Should Support the District Visions to Move the School From Reality to the Vision

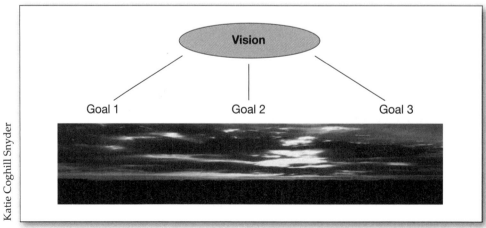

Again, we are talking about the campus vision. The point is to use emerging, recent research and knowledge of systems toward issues such as school improvement processes and strategic planning. In so doing the principal will utilize different kinds of data such as demographic, perceptive, student learning, and processes to collaboratively develop a shared campus vision and a plan for implementing the vision.

C. *Facilitates the collaborative development of a plan that clearly articulates objectives and strategies for implementing a campus vision.*

We are back to the principal's role as facilitator. Remember, it is not the principal's job to do everything. It is the principal's job to see that everything gets done. In this way the principal facilitates the collaborative development of a plan that clearly articulates, or communicates, the objectives and strategies for implementing the campus vision. Figure 5.3 graphically shows how all daily activities should be pursuant to a campus goal and also to the campus vision.

FIGURE 5.3   Activities Should Be Clearly Aligned and Articulated to the Campus and District Vision

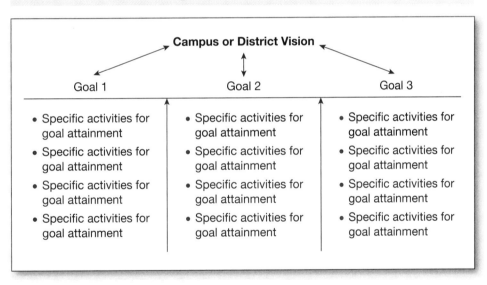

D. *Aligns financial, human, and material resources to support implementation of a campus vision and mission.*

In this descriptor the first part leads directly to the last part. The principal first aligns financial, human, and material resources. Why? To support implementation of a campus vision and mission. In other words, there are certain things that are needed to support the vision and mission of the campus. See to it that they are available.

E. *Establishes procedures to assess and modify implementation plans to promote achievement of the campus vision.*

Sometimes schools, as well as other organizations, have a habit of keeping on doing certain things or programs because, "We've always done it that way before."

Here we assess all school programs and procedures to ensure they are cost efficient (worth what we are putting into them) and doing what they are supposed to be accomplishing versus "We've always done it that way before."

It is time to assess and modify established programs and procedures to make them better, to enhance teaching and learning, and to increase student success. The phrase now becomes "But we've never done it THAT way before!" In so doing we are establishing procedures to assess and modify current implementation plans to promote, or encourage, achievement of the campus vision.

> F.   *Models and promotes the continuous and appropriate development of all stakeholders in the school community to shape the campus culture.*

Sometimes teachers and other stakeholders want to help shape the campus culture in a positive manner, but don't really know how. It is the principal's responsibility to be a role model to everyone regarding how it is done. Further, the principal must promote and encourage appropriate development of all stakeholders such that everyone can work together to collaboratively shape the campus culture.

> G.   **Establishes and communicates consistent expectations for all stakeholders, providing supportive feedback to promote a positive campus environment.**

It is human nature. Everyone needs a pat on the back now and then. Teachers are no different. Make opportunities to give out "Atta Boys!" or "Atta Girls!' as often as possible. They cost nothing, but they do support a positive campus environment.

It is the principal's role to create and communicate consistent expectations for all stakeholders. No one should have a higher or lower performance standard than anyone else. There must never be any "favorites." The expectations for everyone should be high. High expectations is a Sherry, and for good reason. If you don't reach a high goal, it is better than setting a mediocre goal and reaching it with no challenge. Along the way, the principal must give supportive feedback, not "gotcha" feedback, to all stakeholders so they will consistently know how they are doing at all times as well as what their strengths and weaknesses are. If a principal does all these things, it will help promote campus positive environment.

> H.   **Implements effective strategies to systematically gather input from all campus stakeholders, supporting innovative thinking and an inclusive culture.**

Effective teaching strategies and gathering input from all campus stakeholders are essential elements for an effective and productive learning environment. While doing this, principals must encourage and support innovative "out of the box" thinking toward all issues in the school to enhance having an inclusive culture. Remember, if you keep on doing what you have always done, you will keep on getting what you have always gotten. If you are content with the status quo, you will have difficulty working this into your leadership style. However, if you want to pass the TExES exam, you should start believing in this real quick.

I. *Creates an atmosphere of safety that encourages the social, emotional, and physical well-being of staff and students.*

When most of us were children initiatives toward school safety were largely limited to fire drills. Sadly, today we have school bombers, shooters, terrorist activities, and noncustodial parents creating problems. All these issues must have a plan to address them, and they should be practiced, because the likelihood of any of them happening is no longer that far-fetched.

Because of all this, the principal must create an atmosphere where all stakeholders feel safe. This climate should encourage the social, emotional, and physical well-being of all staff and students.

J. *Facilitates the implementation of research-based theories and techniques to promote a campus environment and culture that is conducive to effective teaching and learning and supports organizational health and morale.*

There are always new "bandwagon" ideas for instructional strategies with exceptional claims. If you will just buy their product, all your problems will be solved.

But they never are. There is always a new bandwagon coming around the corner. If all we did was chase bandwagons, we'd never make any forward progress.

So what are you supposed to do to improve student performance?

Implement research-based theories and techniques to promote an effective campus environment and culture. Always stick with initiatives that are research-based. You can never go wrong if you stick with what has been research proven. They will lead the campus environment and culture to effective teaching and learning and will support organizational health and morale.

PRIORITIZED STATEMENTS FOR 001

A. *Creates a positive, collaborative, and collegial campus culture that sets high expectations and facilitates the implementation and achievement of campus initiatives and goals.*

G. *Establishes and communicates consistent expectations for all stakeholders, providing supportive feedback to promote a positive campus environment.*

H. *Implements effective strategies to systematically gather input from all campus stakeholders, supporting innovative thinking and an inclusive culture.*

I. *Creates an atmosphere of safety that encourages the social, emotional, and physical well-being of staff and students.*

IMPORTANT POINTS TO REMEMBER

- Creating a positive and collaborative school culture and climate are essentials.

- Stick with research-based strategies and initiatives.

- As much as possible, keep your school safe!

- Develop a vision with a full set of goals, objectives, and strategies to support it.

CHAPTER 6
Learner-Centered Leadership With Stakeholders

iStock/dszc

Striving for success without hard work is like trying to harvest what you haven't planted.

—David Bly

Domain I: School Culture

Domain Key Concepts: School and Community Leadership

Competency 002

> *The beginning principal knows how to work with stakeholders as key partners to support student learning.*

It is imperative that the school principal knows how to work with all stakeholders as key partners to support student learning. Stakeholders are beyond teachers and staff. They are parents and the entire community itself. Everyone from all segments of the community should be sought after and communicated with to the point that they feel invested in your school. Strongly encourage parents, and others, as volunteers. Even if a volunteer comes to the school and simply listens to a child read, a bond is created between the adult and child, which serves them both well. It also helps the child with their reading. So involve parents and community members as much as possible in the life of the school. There is an old adage that says, "No man is an island." Well, no school is an island either. We need us all working together for the school to maximize its productivity toward student outcomes.

THE PRINCIPAL KNOWS HOW TO . . .

A. *Acknowledges, recognizes, and celebrates the contributions of all stakeholders toward the realization of the campus vision.*

As stated above, everyone in the school community is essential to the success of the school. The success of the school is measured by student learning, which, regretfully, is too heavily based on standardized test scores. These tests are constructed to measure student learning in various content areas per grade level.

Many people must be aligned and working in synchronization such that the learning process works like a well-oiled machine. Then, when test scores come in, as well as along the way, the contributions of all the stakeholders should be not just acknowledged, but moved up on Bloom's Taxonomy to include actual recognition and celebration of the wonderful things that have been accomplished throughout the process.

So the moral of this story is to appreciate and recognize every employee and volunteer involved so they will know that you know they are working hard and are appreciated.

FIGURE 6.1   All Stakeholders Are Important

Utilize All Stakeholders to Maximize Student Learning

- Collaborating with families and other stakeholders

- Responding to community interests and needs

- Mobilizing community resources

Brandy Hudgins

B. *Implements strategies to ensure the development of collegial relationships and effective collaboration.*

This one sounds easy, but isn't. Try taking a group of people who don't particularly like each other and turn them into a collegial group that just loves to collaborate. Even Jesus had trouble with that!

This is an ideal issue to take before your Site-Based Leadership Team, asking for input and problem solving. Remember, it is not your job to do everything alone. But it is your job to see to it that everything gets done. This includes working with multiple constituencies to see to it that everything gets done—including learning to work effectively and collegially together with a sincere focus on student learning and planning strategies that will help guarantee the classroom and school culture and climate improve. Always keep your eyes on the vision of the school. Do everything in relation to obtaining that vision, which certainly should include improving differentiating instruction to meet the individual needs of all students.

C. *Uses consensus-building, conflict-management, communication, and information gathering strategies to involve various stakeholders in planning processes that enable the collaborative development of a shared campus vision and mission focused on teaching and learning.*

This one is a mouthful, so we are going to break it down piece by piece. First, you must use consensus-building, conflict-management, communication, and information gathering strategies with various stakeholders. Remember, who are our stakeholders? Everyone in, near, and around your school! Everyone should be involved. You may say I am dreaming. I say, I don't care. If you don't shoot for the moon, how can you ever reach it?

Next, you must use these stakeholders in all your planning such that they all are involved in the collaborative development of a shared vision and mission of learning that stays constantly focused on teaching and learning. That's what we are about. Teaching and learning. As we work together, collaboratively, we become stronger. We help each other. This is how we build winners in student performance.

Together.

D. *Ensures that parents and other members of the community are an integral part of the campus culture.*

This goes hand-in-hand with element A. Whereas A was about rewarding stakeholders for the parts they played in fulfilling the campus vision, in D you are making sure, ensuring, that parents and other members of the community, indeed, are an important part of this. We need these people to maximize our productivity as it relates to student learning. Practice your reflective thinking. Work with your Site-Based Team and develop strategies that will entice parents and other community members to feel welcome and want to be at the school helping wherever they are needed. If you can accomplish that, you can do anything.

FIGURE 6.2 Families Are Important in the Education of Their Children

Douglas Rife

PRIORITIZED STATEMENTS

C. *Uses consensus-building, conflict-management, communication, and information gathering strategies to involve various stakeholders in planning processes that enable the collaborative development of a shared campus vision and mission focused on teaching and learning.*

D. *Ensures that parents and other members of the community are an integral part of the campus culture.*

IMPORTANT POINTS TO REMEMBER

- Involve everyone in campus decision making and becoming an important part of the campus organization.

- It is not your job to do everything. It is your job to ensure everything gets done.

- Build consensus and not division among all stakeholders.

CHAPTER 7
Learner-Centered Leadership in High-Quality Instruction

Opportunities are usually disguised as hard work so most people don't recognize them.

—Ann Landers

Domain II: Leading Learning

Domain Key Concepts: Instruction, Teaching Effectiveness, and Student Achievement

Competency 003

The beginning principal knows how to collaboratively develop and implement high-quality instruction.

For any school to be highly effective the principal must know how to lead collaboratively developed and implemented high-quality instruction. How to do this is described below.

THE PRINCIPAL KNOWS HOW TO . . .

A. *Prioritizes instruction and student achievement by understanding, sharing, and promoting a clear definition of high-quality instruction based on best practices from recent research.*

All curriculum and instruction should be research-based and built off best practice. Fly-by-night, fix all your problems overnight schemes are usually just that—schemes that are rarely effective. Instructional practices that are based off current research help prioritize student achievement by understanding, sharing, and promoting a clear definition of high-quality instruction. That is what we want: high-quality, research-based instruction that will maximize student instruction and outcomes. We do not need any more quick fixes. As long as an instructional practice is research-based and/or based on best practices, we are good to go. The important point is to know the difference.

> B. *Facilitates the use of sound, research-based practice in the development, implementation, coordination, and evaluation of campus curricular programs to fulfill academic, development, social, and cultural needs.*

FIGURE 7.1   Improving the Process for Greater Student Achievement

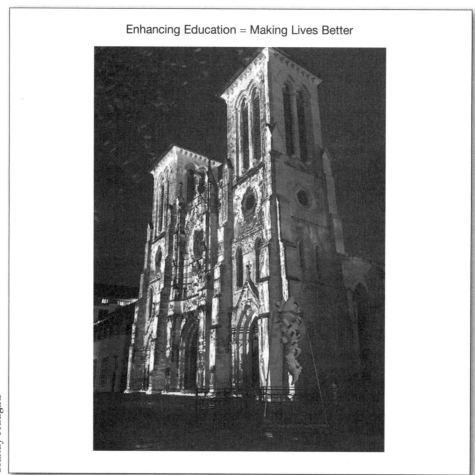

Enhancing Education = Making Lives Better

Brandy Hudgins

The premise here is that campus curricular programs should enhance the academic, development, social, and cultural needs of the students. Again, sound, research-based practices should be developed, implemented, coordinated, and evaluated to meet these same goals. Basically, we want all our programs to be *aligned* with their academic, developmental, social, and cultural needs. Actually, everything we do in schools should be *aligned* with the needs of the students. If something is not, why are we doing it?

> C. *Facilitates campus participation in collaborative district planning, implementation, monitoring, and revision of the curriculum to ensure appropriate scope, sequence, content, and alignment.*

There are three components to this.

1. Facilitating campus participation in virtually everything,

2. But especially toward district planning, implementation, monitoring, and revision of the curriculum. Why?

3. To ensure appropriate scope, sequence, content, and alignment.

The third portion is particularly important. It is essential that you know the correct definitions of the terms. Scope refers to the big picture of the curriculum or anything else. Sequence is what we are focusing on now and in what order. For example, the quadratic equation is a sequential piece of algebra, but it is not the full scope of what algebra is all about.

The content is what material and/or lessons are to be covered, while alignment means everything taught is in line with something else such as a campus goal. It is important that everything be aligned with something in the schools' philosophical base, vision, or mission. Again, if it does not, why are we teaching it?

FIGURE 7.2   Facilitating Top Instruction

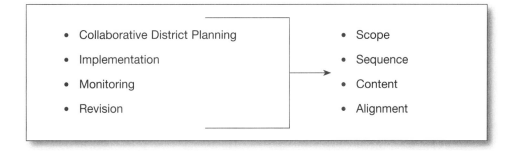

- Collaborative District Planning
- Implementation
- Monitoring
- Revision

- Scope
- Sequence
- Content
- Alignment

> D. *Implements a rigorous curriculum that is aligned with state standards, including college and career-readiness standards.*

For various reasons, not every student is headed to college. Some are headed to vocational schools. It is our role to prepare both sets of students for each of their goals. The curriculum in both curriculums should be rigorous and should be aligned, or focused, on some campus goal or state standard including both college and career-readiness standards. No program should be continued by, "But we've always done it that way before." Evaluate it and everything else. If it does not prove to enhance learning, or is not cost effective, it is time to try something else. The state standards upon which the TExES domains and competencies are built are shown in Addendum A.

> E. *Facilitates the use and integration of technology, telecommunications, and information systems to enhance learning.*

The days of slide rules are gone. Today everything is done via technology. Even the scheduling of classes is done via technology. The world has changed. Students must graduate being computer savvy regardless of where they are going after graduation. Therefore, the integration of technology, telecommunications, and information systems to enhance learning are truly essential elements across the curriculum. Your job is not to teach technology. It is your job to see to it that the technology teachers have everything they need to be able to teach the most current of trends effectively.

PRIORITIZED STATEMENTS

> A. ***Prioritizes instruction and student achievement by understanding, sharing, and promoting a clear definition of high-quality instruction based on best practices from recent research.***
>
> B. ***Facilitates the use of sound, research-based practice in the development, implementation, coordination, and evaluation of campus curricular programs to fulfill academic, development, social, and cultural needs.***
>
> C. ***Facilitates campus participation in collaborative district planning, implementation, monitoring, and revision of the curriculum to ensure appropriate scope, sequence, content, and alignment.***
>
> D. ***Implements a rigorous curriculum that is aligned with state standards, including college and career-readiness standards.***

IMPORTANT POINTS TO REMEMBER

- Keep everything aligned.
- Make clear and measurable goals with deadlines.
- Provide high-quality curriculum and instruction.
- Collaborate with virtually everyone about virtually everything!

CHAPTER 8

Learner-Centered Leadership in Promoting Teacher Effectiveness and Student Achievement

iStock/dszc

It doesn't matter where you have been. It only matters where you are going.

—**Brian Tracy**

Domain II: Leading Learning

Domain Key Concepts: Instructional Leadership, Teaching, and Learning

Competency 004

The beginning principal knows how to monitor and assess classroom instruction to promote teacher effectiveness and student achievement.

There is significant overlap among the competencies. For example, we have discussed, or will discuss, Instruction, Teacher Effectiveness, and Student Achievement elsewhere. This overlap is not a contradiction. It is a reiteration of the importance of these concepts. In this competency we are looking at these concepts from the perspective of Learner-Centered Leadership in Promoting Teacher Effectiveness and Student Achievement.

THE PRINCIPAL KNOWS HOW TO . . .

A. *Monitors instruction routinely by visiting classrooms, observing instruction, and attending grade-level, department, or team meetings to provide evidence-based feedback to improve instruction.*

It's all about being visible and paying attention to what is going on in classrooms. Some people have an incorrect perception of a principal just sitting in an office all day tending to paperwork.

Wrong.

Highly effective principals spend little time in their offices during the traditional work day. Instead, they are visiting and observing in classrooms, attending grade-level or content area meetings, conducting official and unofficial walk-throughs, for the purpose of providing evidence-based feedback to improve instruction and, thus, student achievement. This cannot occur when the principal is closed off in the office. How can an *instructional leader* be an *instructional* leader when he or she is never in a classroom? It's not possible. Therefore, get out of that office and into the halls, cafeteria, and classrooms. Be interactive and helpful. Be the instructional leader you were meant to be.

FIGURE 8.1 Provide Consistent Feedback With High Expectations

Michael Whitney

B. *Analyzes the curriculum collaboratively to guide teachers in aligning content across grades and ensures that curricular scopes and sequences meet the needs of their diverse student populations (considering sociological, linguistic, cultural, and other factors).*

As the instructional leader of the campus, the principal utilizes stakeholders collaboratively to guide, or assist, teachers in aligning curriculum across grade levels. As a part of this, the curriculum must provide scope and sequences that meet the needs of all their students, stressing the importance of a diverse, or different, population. This includes, in part, students from different sociological, linguistic, cultural, and other factors. Since they list "other factors," the door is open to anything and everything that could impact teaching and/or learning.

FIGURE 8.2   Multiple Sources of Data

Monitor, Analyze, and Ensure the Use of Multiple Forms of Data

Greg Wilmore

C. *Monitors and ensures staff use multiple forms of student data to inform instruction and intervention decisions that maximizes instructional effectiveness and student achievement.*

All teachers should use more than one form of assessment to guide their instruction and interventions for low points in student learning. In other words, although the STARR test is important, it should not be the *only* form of assessment used to guide instruction and interventions. Multiple sources of data should be utilized including daily work and various observations. The point is to use every single bit of information (data) possible to maximize instructional effectiveness and student achievement.

D. *Promotes instruction that supports the growth of individual students and student groups, supports equity, and works to reduce the achievement gap.*

Effective principals encourage instruction that supports the growth of individual students (e.g., individualized instruction, differentiated instruction). Teaching to the individual child's needs is imperative to maximize student success. However, this also applies to student groups as well.

Supporting student equity and the differences among students cannot be overstated. Today's classrooms are more diverse than any time in our nation's history. The same old instructional techniques that have been used for years may, or may not, work today. It is the principal's job to see to it that teachers have the resources they need to make learning relevant to all students and, frankly, the desire to do so. The principal, therefore, supports equity both in talk and in actions. There is a solid focus to reduce any achievement gaps among any subgroups. The goal is for every student to maximize his or her learning potential and to have teachers devoted and having the appropriate skills to make this happen.

E. *Supports staff in developing the capacity and time to collaboratively and individually use classroom formative and summative assessment data to inform effective instructional practices and interventions.*

It is the responsibility of the principal to support teachers in all facets of the school, but particularly regarding academics. After all, academics are our primary function. Even among the most intentional of principals, find time for faculty and staff to have the capacity to individually think about and reflect on both formative and summative assessment to improve their instructional practices and the interventions they utilize for individual students as needed.

PRIORITIZED STATEMENTS

A. *Monitors instruction routinely by visiting classrooms, observing instruction, and attending grade-level, department, or team meetings to provide evidence-based feedback to improve instruction.*

B. *Analyzes the curriculum collaboratively to guide teachers in aligning content across grades and ensures that curricular scopes and sequences meet the needs of their diverse student populations (considering sociological, linguistic, cultural, and other factors).*

C. *Monitors and ensures staff use multiple forms of student data to inform instruction and intervention decisions that maximizes instructional effectiveness and student achievement.*

D. *Promotes instruction that supports the growth of individual students and student groups, supports equity, and works to reduce the achievement gap.*

E. *Supports staff in developing the capacity and time to collaboratively and individually use classroom formative and summative assessment data to inform effective instructional practices and interventions.*

IMPORTANT POINTS TO REMEMBER

- ALL students are important, and ALL students deserve our best in meeting their individual needs.
- Get out of the office and into classrooms.
- All curriculum should be aligned across grades and content areas.
- All goals should be aligned with the campus vision.
- All goals must have strategies to support them.
- It is imperative that everything be done to increase student learning and outcomes.

CHAPTER 9
Learner-Centered Leadership Through Professional Development

The way to get started is to quit talking and begin doing.

—**Walt Disney**

Domain III: Human Capital

Domain Key Concepts: Professional Development, HR Management, and Personnel and Self-Appraisal

Competency 005

> *The beginning principal knows how to provide feedback, coaching, and professional development to staff through evaluation and supervision, knows how to reflect on his/her own practice, and strives to grow professionally.*

If I had to pick a single competency that basically covers everything, this would be it. Read it slowly and carefully for comprehension. Then proceed to the following six descriptors. Then you will be ready to rock through the following 10 competencies. But first, make sure you understand exactly what Competency 001 is saying to you.

THE PRINCIPAL KNOWS HOW TO . . .

A. *Communicates expectations to staff and uses multiple data points (e.g., regular observations, walk-throughs, teacher and student data, and other sources) to complete evidence-based evaluations of all staff.*

Faculty and staff must have a clear understanding of the principal's expectations for them in detail beyond helping all students learn. Otherwise it is like taking a trip without a map. Therefore, you must clearly articulate your expectations toward the use of all data points such as regular classroom observations, walk-throughs, teacher and student data, and any other resources necessary to complete evidence-based evaluations of all staff. You may not get rid of someone just because you don't care for them. There is this thing called due process for teachers that must be addressed. Also, all your various evaluative data should be in writing. Every attempt reasonably possible should be made to utilize evidence-based evaluations providing ways for teachers to improve their instructional strategies for the ultimate goal of increasing student outcomes.

FIGURE 9.1   Use Data From Multiple Sources in Decision Making

Patti Dahlstrom

B. *Coaches and develops teachers by facilitating teacher self-assessment and goal setting, conducting conferences, giving individualized feedback, and supporting individualized professional growth opportunities.*

The goal here is to promote the highest level of teacher self-reflection and assessment. Hopefully, teachers will use this data as tools to improve their instructional techniques for the benefit of all students. For this to occur, the principal must lead them in personal goal setting by conducting conferences and providing individualized feedback that will support individualized professional growth opportunities. These individual professional growth activities should be based on the needs of the teacher that must, as always, be aligned with the needs of the students.

FIGURE 9.2   Integrated Technology and Vision Alignment

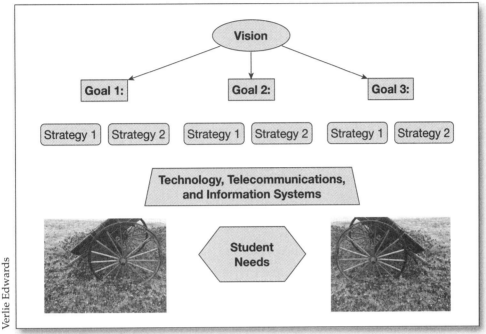

Verlie Edwards

C. *Collaborates to develop, implement, and revise a comprehensive and ongoing plan for the professional development of campus staff that addresses staff needs based on staff appraisal trends, goals, and student information/data.*

Descriptor C is a close cousin of Descriptor B. This one focuses on professional development, but this time it is about staff appraisal trends, goals, and more student information/data. This includes, but is not limited to, state testing scores. It should include all information regarding this specific teacher's students. This data may be collected from student work samples, walk-throughs, or other sources. The point is to use evidence to create a comprehensive and ongoing professional development plan for campus staff.

D. *Facilitates a continuum of effective professional development activities that includes appropriate content, process, context, allocation of time, funding, and other needed resources.*

Continuing with our focus on professional development, Descriptor D focuses on the scope and sequence process of first having appropriate content followed by a research-based implementation context and process with an appropriate allocation of time, funding, and needed resources. It's all in including all the concepts and not leaving any out.

> E. *Engages in ongoing and meaningful professional growth activities, reflects on his or her practice, seeks and acts on feedback, and strives to continually improve, learn, and grow.*

The principal should facilitate each teacher being engaged in ongoing (continuous) professional growth activities. The activities should include teacher reflection on their own practice. Using that data, the principal should lead teachers to seek and act based on feedback they receive from their reflection and other relevant sources. Last, principals as well as teachers should be life-long learners striving to continually improve, learn, and grow professionally.

> F. *Seeks assistance (e.g., mentor, central office) to ensure effective and reflective decision making and works collaboratively with campus and district leadership.*

In Descriptor F principals are encouraged to not try to go it alone. Seek help from mentors, the central office, and any other sources. Use the feedback, including personal reflection, to make decisions that will actually work. Last, be sure to work collaboratively with campus and district leadership. By using district feedback, you are guaranteed that when it is your own evaluation time, you will have addressed everything that the district office has suggested that you address. Remember, people support what they help create.

PRIORITIZED STATEMENTS

> A. *Communicates expectations to staff and uses multiple data points (e.g., regular observations, walk-throughs, teacher and student data, and other sources) to complete evidence-based evaluations of all staff.*
>
> B. *Coaches and develops teachers by facilitating teacher self-assessment and goal setting, conducting conferences, giving individualized feedback, and supporting individualized professional growth opportunities.*
>
> C. *Collaborates to develop, implement, and revise a comprehensive and ongoing plan for the professional development of campus staff that addresses staff needs based on staff appraisal trends, goals, and student information/data.*
>
> D. *Facilitates a continuum of effective professional development activities that includes appropriate content, process, context, allocation of time, funding, and other needed resources.*

IMPORTANT POINTS TO REMEMBER

- Professional development is a huge element in both your personal development and that of your school.

- Seek feedback for your own professional development from multiple sources including both your staff and the district central office.

- Facilitate collaboration.

- Ensure all staff development, including your own, includes genuine reflection and is aligned with the needs of the teachers and the students themselves.

- Professional development should not be cookie cutter, one size fits all, but aligned with teacher and student needs.

CHAPTER 10

Learner-Centered Leadership Promoting Teacher Excellence and Growth

iStock/dszc

Success is going from failure to failure without a loss of enthusiasm.

—Winston Churchill

Domain III: Human Capital

Domain Key Concepts: Professional Development, Relationships, and Student Outcomes

Competency 006

> *The beginning principal knows how to promote high-quality teaching by using selection, placement, and retention practices to promote teacher excellence and growth.*

It's a cycle. To get good new teachers starts with the selection process itself. Utilize either your Site Based Decision Making Team or the teachers in that content or grade level. Then place them where they are most likely to be successful and bring the highest impact to student outcomes. Finally, through walk-throughs and other forms of evaluation, serve as mentors to promote teacher excellence and growth.

THE PRINCIPAL KNOWS HOW TO . . .

> A. *Invests and manages time to prioritize the development, support, and supervision of the staff to maximize student outcomes.*

It takes time and focused effort to prioritize the development, support, and supervision of the staff to maximize student outcomes, but it is one of the most important roles of a principal. After all, the teachers instruct the classroom, which is where most learning takes place. Time spent on helping teachers grow is time well spent because it will manifest itself in improved student learning.

But just filling out a form and putting it in teachers' boxes for them to sign is not prioritizing their development. A 5-minute post-conference won't cut it either. Both you and the teacher must take the process seriously, looking for ways to improve for even the best teachers. No matter how good, or bad, a teacher is, there is always room for improvement. That's called being a life-long learner, and the process is a priority.

FIGURE 10.1   The Campus Success Flowchart

B. *Facilitates collaborative structures that support professional learning communities in reviewing data, processes, and policies in order to improve teaching and learning in the school.*

This one is a no-brainer. Of course, we should support professional learning communities by reviewing multiple forms of data, various processes in use, and abiding by policies in place to improve both teaching and learning in the school.

C. *Creates leadership opportunities, defines roles, and delegates responsibilities to effective staff and administrators to support campus goal attainment.*

Delegation is a two-headed sword. When it turns out good, it is very good because leaders are being built. But there must be training and clearly defined roles and responsibilities. When those things do not occur, it can be a very bad thing with bedlam reigning. The right hand doesn't know what the left hand is doing or why. That's a communication issue.

So training must take place among all stakeholders to keep the train running toward campus goal attainment rather than chaos. Ensure that everyone knows and understands their roles!

FIGURE 10.2   Timeline of Teacher

Recruitment ⟶ Screening ⟶ Hiring ⟶ Supporting

Mike Hewlett

D. *Implements effective, appropriate, and legal strategies for the recruitment, screening, hiring, assignment, induction, development, evaluation, promotion, retention, discipline, and dismissal of campus staff.*

This one is a true mouthful. Think of it as a line graph. We must implement effective, appropriate, and legal strategies for

- recruitment,

- screening,

- hiring,

- assignment,

- induction,

- development,

- evaluation,

- promotion,

- retention,

- discipline, and

- dismissal of campus staff.

And that, my friends, says it all.

PRIORITIZED STATEMENTS

A. *Invests and manages time to prioritize the development, support, and supervision of the staff to maximize student outcomes.*

B. *Facilitates collaborative structures that support professional learning communities in reviewing data, processes, and policies in order to improve teaching and learning in the school.*

C. *Creates leadership opportunities, defines roles, and delegates responsibilities to effective staff and administrators to support campus goal attainment.*

D. *Implements effective, appropriate, and legal strategies for the recruitment, screening, hiring, assignment, induction, development, evaluation, promotion, retention, discipline, and dismissal of campus staff.*

IMPORTANT POINTS TO REMEMBER

- Prioritize time for the recruitment and development of new teachers.

- Create collaborative structures to support new teachers.

- Delegate, but do it appropriately.

- Support and nurture your staff.

CHAPTER 11

Learner-Centered Leadership Through Communication Skills

iStock/dszc

You have brains in your head, and feet in your shoes.

You can steer yourself in any direction you choose.

—Dr. Seuss

Domain IV: Executive Leadership

Domain Key Concepts: Communication, Relationships, and Improving Student Outcomes

Competency 007

The beginning principal knows how to develop relationships with internal and external stakeholders, including selecting appropriate communication strategies for audiences.

This competency again returns to the concept of improving student outcomes, but it comes at it from the perspective of good communication skills as well as building relationships. Both of these are building blocks to improving student outcomes.

THE PRINCIPAL KNOWS HOW TO . . .

A. ***Understands how to effectively communicate a message in different ways to meet the needs of various audiences.***

Sometimes it is not what you say, but how you say it. So two different people could say the same thing in different ways. One may be accepted, while the other is rejected. There is a direct correlation here with, "No one cares how much you know, until they know how much you care."

Different ways of communication are necessary when speaking to different groups of people. For example, explaining a new campus program could be done differently when a principal is talking to the PTA, the School Board, or the Rotary Club. You base how you communicate with who you are communicating with. It's all about the audience you are speaking to. Regardless, never "talk down" to people. That is a sure way to get them NOT to agree with you! Treat each group with respect and dignity. Therefore, even though you may have to present in different ways to different groups, remember to always be ready, have done your homework, and treat people with respect and dignity.

B. Develops and implements strategies for systematically communicating internally and externally.

When you need to speak to any group, prepare ahead of time. Be ready. Never wing it! Winging it is a sure way to get yourself into trouble and does not allow you to lead the conversation. You need to *nicely* control the situation. Decide what you are going to say, and develop then implement a systematic plan of how to say it regardless if it is either inside or outside the school itself.

C. Develops and implements a comprehensive program of community relations that uses strategies that effectively involve and inform multiple constituencies.

It is necessary to develop and implement a comprehensive program of community relations that you can use with a mere moment's notice. Things happen, and sometimes they happen fast! You need your plan in place for how you will deal with the media and so on that uses strategies that effectively involve and inform multiple constituencies—virtually everyone.

FIGURE 11.1   Everyone Is Necessary to Achieve a Student-Focused Campus Vision

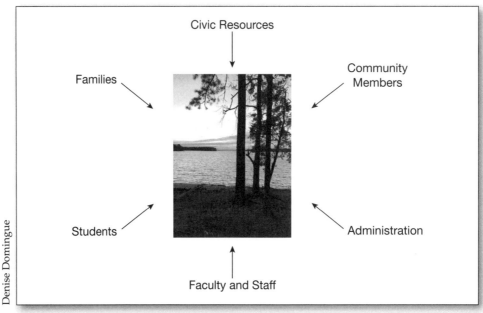

D. *Establishes partnerships with parents, businesses, and other groups in the community to strengthen programs and support campus goals.*

It is vastly important to develop relationships and become partners with parents, businesses, and other groups in the community to strengthen programs and support campus goals. You want them involved in campus decision making. You also want them on your side in case all Hades breaks loose. That's not likely since you are an ideal principal, but it still could happen. You also want these strong partnerships to support campus goals. It is a "together we build" situation. In short, you need these partnerships for a myriad of reasons.

FIGURE 11.2   Partnerships

Establish Partnerships With

- Parents
- Businesses
- Community Groups

Greg Wilmore

PRIORITIZED STATEMENTS

A. *Understands how to effectively communicate a message in different ways to meet the needs of various audiences.*

B. *Develops and implements strategies for systematically communicating internally and externally.*

IMPORTANT POINTS TO REMEMBER

- Build positive relationships!
- Have an effective communications plan!
- Involve the community!

CHAPTER 12

Learner-Centered Leadership in Improving Student Outcomes

iStock/dszc

Education's purpose is to replace an empty mind with an open one.

—**Malcolm Forbes**

Domain IV: Executive Leadership

Domain Key Concepts: Communication, Relationships, and Improving Student Outcomes

Competency 008

The beginning principal knows how to focus on improving student outcomes through organizational collaboration, resiliency, and change management.

In Competency 008 we are still addressing improving student outcomes, but we are coming at it from the perspective of communication skills and relationship building. The descriptors below tell us how.

THE PRINCIPAL KNOWS HOW TO . . .

A. *Demonstrates awareness of social and economic issues that exist within the school and community that affect campus operations and student learning.*

To create positive communication and relationship skills for the purpose of improving students' outcomes, principals must demonstrate, or show, awareness of social and economic issues that exist within the school and community that affect, or even may affect, the operation of the campus and that could have an impact on student learning. Examples could run from highly contested elections to severe weather conditions. Anything that could be a distraction from student total focus on learning would fall in this category. Actually, there isn't much that couldn't fall in this category. Mom and Dad have a big fight that upsets Johnny? This category. No food in the house? This category. One parent is in jail and the other is doing drugs? This category. It is vast and widespread. Anything that impacts a child, impacts their learning.

> B. *Gathers and organizes information from a variety of sources to facilitate creative thinking, critical thinking, and problem solving to guide effective campus decision making.*

There are two parts to this descriptor. The first regards gathering and organizing information (data) from a variety of sources. The more information you have on any child or situation, the better informed your decision making will be. Obviously, this will include Texas' Big Tests. But it goes beyond that to student daily work, classroom observations, conferencing with both teachers and parents, and so on. You want as much data as possible to make a better informed decision.

The second part of this descriptor is the "why" you need all this data to make informed decisions. The data will facilitate you with creative thinking, critical thinking, and problem solving to guide you in making effective campus decision making. Remember that even the smallest decisions at the time can easily mushroom into large impacts down the road. Therefore, *every* decision is important.

> C. **Frames, analyses, and creatively resolves campus problems using effective problem-solving techniques to make timely, high-quality decisions.**

C is similar to B in many ways, which is why they are both in Competency 008. However, this descriptor comes at problem solving from a different perspective. Here we are thinking a problem through by framing, analyzing, and creatively resolving problems to be able to make timely, high-quality decisions. In B we were looking at the data. Here we are using problem-solving skills and creativity to do the same thing. Your choice is not an either-or. It is both. Utilize both techniques to make prudent decisions.

> D. *Develops, implements, and evaluates systems and processes for organizational effectiveness to keep staff inspired and focused on the campus vision.*

Often teachers can come back to school after their summer break pumped up to really get things done. But as time goes by they wear out. They get just plain tired.

This descriptor is about keeping them pumped up when they are far from pumped up. This does not mean they are bad teachers. It just means they are tired teachers. It is your role to inspire them in every reasonable way possible to keep on keeping on working steadfastly toward the campus vision. So you develop, implement, and evaluate models to do just that. Some will work, while some won't. But you won't know till you try then evaluating everything you have done. Remember, "How can I make it better?" is the number-one question in school leadership and in life.

> E. *Uses effectively planning, time management, and organization of work to support attainment of school district and campus goals.*

In the simplest of terms, this means to get your act together and keep it together. No school needs a disorganized principal. If it is not your thing to keep your office tidy, learn. No one can maximize their productivity in a mess. Organize your work, often by projects. Everything should have a place and be in that place unless you are working on it at that moment. Organize your time also. Trivia can eat up your entire day, yet you would have nothing to show for it.

One way to do this is every day before you go home: make a list of all you need to accomplish the next day including walk-throughs. Some may be things you needed to do today, but simply ran out of time. Once you have your list, prioritize it. Then leave it on top of your *clean* desk where it will welcome you the next morning.

Of course, things will come up (too often) to keep you from completing your list, but at the end of the day, you can roll over to tomorrow's list of things that didn't get done today. By having an ongoing To Do list, you will maximize your productivity and never forget something major or minor that you are supposed to do. Have a To Do list in your personal life also, and for the same reasons. I have a To Do list every single day of my life. It's become a habit, but it is a good habit that keeps me on track with all the many things I have to do. I encourage you to make it a habit both professionally and personally also. A To Do list will eventually take you, and your campus, to your goals.

PRIORITIZED STATEMENTS

> C. *Frames, analyses, and creatively resolves campus problems using effective problem-solving techniques to make timely, high-quality decisions.*

> E. *Uses effectively planning, time management, and organization of work to support attainment of school district and campus goals.*

IMPORTANT POINTS TO REMEMBER

- Pay attention to what is going on around you.
- Be a problem solver.
- Make data-driven decisions.
- Involve both the school community and the school itself.

CHAPTER 13
Learner-Centered Leadership in Goal Setting

iStock/dszc

Always do right. This will surprise some people and astonish the rest.

—Mark Twain

Domain V: Strategic Operations

Domain Key Concepts: Goals, Strategies, and a Safe and Nurturing Learning Environment

Competency 009

The beginning principal knows how to collaboratively determine goals and implement strategies aligned with the school vision that support teacher effectiveness and positive student outcomes.

Collaboration with the entire school community (e.g., all stakeholders) is key to determining campus goals and aligning them with the school vision. The school vision must support teacher effectiveness and positive student outcomes. Without these things happening, you do not have goals. You have dreams.

THE PRINCIPAL KNOWS HOW TO . . .

A. *Assesses the current needs of the campus, analyzing a wide set of evidence to determine campus objectives, and sets measurable school goals, targets, and strategies that form the school's strategic plan.*

This is a step-by-step descriptor. First, you and your campus team must assess the need of the campus based on student performance data. Once the needs have been determined, analyze all the available data and assessment points to determine campus objectives. These objectives should support attainment of one or more campus goal, targets, and strategies that form the school's Strategic, or Campus Improvement, Plan.

FIGURE 13.1   Strategic Planning

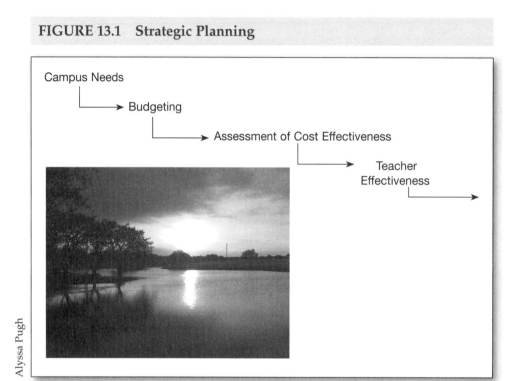

B. *Establishes structures that outline and track the progress using multiple data points and makes adjustments as needed to improve teacher effectiveness and student outcomes.*

Through collaboration create an outline that provides for tracking progress through the use of data points. Thus, make adjustments as needed at any time during the year to improve teacher effectiveness, which, in turn, will lead to enhanced student outcomes. Assessment should be continuous, not just when regular benchmarks are given. Continuous assessment is an important TExES concept.

C. *Allocates resources effectively (e.g., staff time, master schedule, dollars, and tools), aligning them with school objectives and goals, and works to access additional resources as needed to support learning.*

FIGURE 13.2   The Budget and the Vision Must Support Each Other

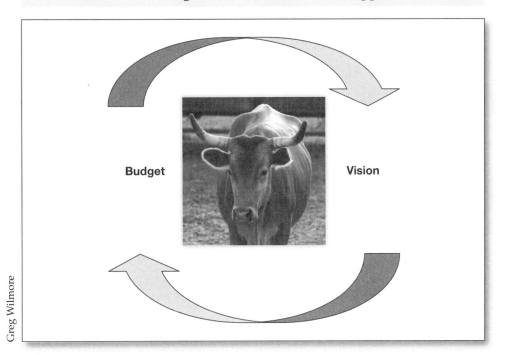

Greg Wilmore

Budget   Vision

All resources should be allocated, or distributed, aligned, or lined up with school objectives and goals for the purpose of working to access additional resources as needed to support student learning. Again, all resources should be aligned with the needs of the students. *Everything* we do or have should be aligned with the needs of the students. If not, why not?

> D. *Implements appropriate management techniques and group processes to define roles, assign functions, delegate authority, and determine accountability for campus goal attainment.*

Everything done should be defined, and everyone should understand their unique responsibility toward their part of it. Thus, everyone is held accountable for their own responsibilities without exception. For this to happen, the principal must implement appropriate management techniques and group processes to define exactly what everyone's roles, assigned functions, authority, and determination for accountability is for the attainment of campus goals. This is called teamwork.

PRIORITIZED STATEMENTS

> A. ***Assesses the current needs of the campus, analyzing a wide set of evidence to determine campus objectives, and sets measurable school goals, targets, and strategies that form the school's strategic plan.***

B. *Establishes structures that outline and track the progress using multiple data points and makes adjustments as needed to improve teacher effectiveness and student outcomes.*

C. *Allocates resources effectively (e.g., staff time, master schedule, dollars, and tools), aligning them with school objectives and goals, and works to access additional resources as needed to support learning.*

IMPORTANT POINTS TO REMEMBER

- Work as a team!

- Everyone understands their roles and responsibilities in all tasks toward campus goal attainment.

- Accountability structures should be put in place.

CHAPTER 14

Learner-Centered Administrative Leadership

iStock/dszc

Good management consists in showing average people how to do the work of superior people.

—**John D. Rockefeller**

Domain V: Strategic Operations

Domain Key Concepts: Ethics, Student Advocacy, and Ensuring Success for All Learners

Competency 010

> *The beginning principal knows how to provide administrative leadership through resource management, policy implementation, and coordination of school operations and programs to ensure a safe learning environment.*

This competency is exactly what it says it is: Administrative Leadership. It does not directly relate to curriculum or instruction. As David Erlandson of Texas A&M University, College Station, says, "It's hard to keep your eyes on the vision of the school when the walls are falling down." That pretty much sums up this entire competency. It is assessing your management of the campus skills. After all, someone must keep the walls of the school from falling.

THE PRINCIPAL KNOWS HOW TO . . .

A. *Implements strategies that enable the physical plant, equipment, and support systems to operate safely, efficiently, and effectively to maintain a conducive learning environment.*

To have a conducive, or nurturing, learning environment for stakeholders, certain things must be taking place. Principals must implement, or put into place, strategies that enable and/or help the physical plant, school equipment, and support systems such as the heating and air conditioning to improve and maintain a nurturing learning environment. A nurturing learning environment includes both the culture and climate of the campus. It is all the things that make students feel safe and comfortable enough to learn. Further, all this must be done and operated safely, efficiently, and effectively to maintain a conducive learning environment.

FIGURE 14.1   Student Safety Is Paramount

Katie Coghill Snyder

B. *Applies strategies for ensuring the safety of students and personnel and for addressing emergencies and security concerns, including developing and implementing a crisis plan.*

School safety is of the highest importance. All your questions related to any form of student and/or staff safety are from this descriptor. Therefore, principals must create and implement strategies for making sure the students and personnel are safe at all times. These strategies must also address emergencies and security concerns including developing and implementing a crisis plan. Input should be gotten from the district itself as well as the local police department. The Crisis Management Plan should also be aligned with the District Crisis Management Plan.

Regretfully, we are having more and more school shootings. We absolutely *must* come up with crisis management plans that are both proactive and reactive in protecting our students, faculty, and staff. It should be collaboratively developed, and it should be *practiced*. We cannot control the idiots who are out to harm our schools. But we can control being prepared to protect our people as much as is humanly possible.

C. *Applies local, state, and federal laws and policies to support sound decisions while considering implications related to all school operations and programs (e.g., student services, food services, health services, and transportation).*

This is the "Keep It Legal" descriptor. The principal absolutely must apply all local, state, and federal laws and policies to support sound decisions regardless. Even if the law appears crazy or a policy seems nonsensical, principals must follow them unless, or until, they are changed. Otherwise, laws and policies that are in place are in stone. These laws and policies include those that are related to all operations and programs including student services, food services, health services, transportation, and anything else that has laws, policies, or rules attached to it. All you must remember is "Keep it legal!" You can never get in trouble if you follow the rules, even when the rules appear goofy.

FIGURE 14.2   Law and Policy Provide a School's Basic Operating Structure

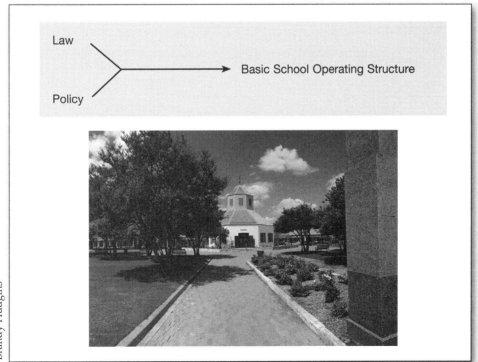

Brandy Hudgins

> D. *Collaboratively plans and effectively manages the campus budget within state law and district policies to promote sound financial management in relation to accounts, bidding, purchasing, and grants.*

The budget is another area that can get you in trouble really quick. Some basic things to remember are:

- It should be developed collaboratively based on the needs of the students.

- Once it is approved by both the central office and the entire School Board, it becomes real. Until then, it is just what you hope it will be.

- Once it is real and you have it, stay in it.

- Do not overspend in any category. If you do overspend in various categories too many times, the superintendent will solve that problem for you. He or she will replace you with someone who can consistently add and subtract.

All this is summed up in Descriptor D. It also says the budget should be planned collaboratively and managed effectively. (Remember how to add and subtract.) All campus and the district's budget must be within state law and district policies such that the budget promotes and supports effective financial management. Some areas to be sure to have sound financial management are accounts, bidding and purchasing, which are mainly done out of the central office, and grants. Just remember to keep everything transparently legal. If a potential purchase even smells a little bit "iffy," don't do it. It could come back to bite you. Be careful!

> E. *Uses technology to enhance school management (e.g., attendance systems, teacher grade books, shared drives, and grants).*

Technology is more of a focus on 268 than it was in 068. In addition to using technology to enhance the curriculum, it also should be used to enhance, or make better, school management. This includes attendance systems, teacher grade books, shared drives, grants, and anything else that improves the operation of the school.

> F. *Facilitates the effective coordination of campus curricular, cocurricular, and extracurricular programs in relation to other school district programs to fulfil the academic, developmental, social, and cultural needs of students.*

Obviously, the primary function of a school is teaching and learning. But we cannot stop with just that. There is another side to a balanced education. That side includes cocurricular and extracurricular programs.

Effective principals coordinate all these with the academic purposes of the school to fulfil the developmental, social, and other cultural needs of all the students.

> G. *Collaborate with district staff to ensure the understanding and implementation of district policies and advocates for the needs of students and staff.*

We have discussed the importance of knowing and staying within district policies several times. Since they keep coming back to it, you can bet they think it is important. If they think it is important, so do we! Therefore, effective principals must collaborate closely with district level staff to make sure they understand and implement district policies to advocate for the needs of all the students and staff. Frankly, it is better to just stay in the policies rather than get in trouble with no defense. They are there in black and white. Read them. If you don't understand them, speak up! Ask questions! Don't let yourself be caught in the trap of messing up simply because you either did not know a policy existed or did not know what it meant.

> H. **Implements strategies for student discipline and attendance in a manner that ensures student safety, consistency, and equity and that legal requirements are met (e.g., due process SPED requirements).**

The last areas, and very important ones, that we must address in Administrative Leadership are student discipline and attendance. We must get attendance right for state attendance and funding requirements. That is nonnegotiable.

Student discipline is a different story. It finds you. Students are different today than in the past. They have less respect for the school as an institution and toward educators as leaders. Many, frankly, just don't care.

So they make trouble. It can be large or small, but it is still trouble. Then you are left to deal with it.

Great. Just what you got your master's degree for. Solving discipline problems.

You have no idea how I wish I could give you a nice, simple solution to discipline problems so you would not have to deal with them.

On the other side of the coin, we can never fully know what exactly those same kids are dealing with at home—and bringing with them to school.

With this background, you can more clearly understand Descriptor H, which encourages us to implement strategies to resolve student discipline and attendance in a way that guarantees student safety, consistency, equity, and that legal requirements are met, particularly regarding due process (It must occur) and SPED requirements (Anything decided in an Admission, Review, and Dismissal [ARD] committee meeting and put in a student's Individual Education Plan [IEP] is like law until another ARD can be held that determines different results).

PRIORITIZED STATEMENTS

B. *Applies strategies for ensuring the safety of students and personnel and for addressing emergencies and security concerns, including developing and implementing a crisis plan.*

C. *Applies local, state, and federal laws and policies to support sound decisions while considering implications related to all school operations and programs (e.g., student services, food services, health services, and transportation).*

D. *Collaboratively plans and effectively manages the campus budget within state law and district policies to promote sound financial management in relation to accounts, bidding, purchasing, and grants.*

H. *Implements strategies for student discipline and attendance in a manner that ensures student safety, consistency, and equity and that legal requirements are met (e.g., due process SPED requirements).*

IMPORTANT POINTS TO REMEMBER

- Follow all policies and laws, even if you don't like them.
- Build your budget collaboratively, and stay in it.
- Have a Crisis Management Plan, and practice it regularly.
- Keep everything legal!

CHAPTER 15

Learner-Centered Ethical and Equitable Leadership

iStock/dszc

A wise man will make more opportunities than he finds.

—Sir Francis Bacon

Domain VI: Ethics, Equity, and Diversity

Domain Key Concepts: Ethics, Student Advocacy, and Ensuring Success for All Learners

Competency 011

> *The beginning principal knows how to provide ethical leadership by advocating for children and ensuring student access to effective educators, programs, and services.*

THE PRINCIPAL KNOWS HOW TO . . .

> A. *Implements policies and procedures that require all campus personnel to comply with the Educators' Code of Ethics (TAC Chapter 247).*

They have never asked students to quote this or to identify phrases from it. However, this is a new test so they could. My suggestions are to Google the Educators Code of Ethics cited above, or tell me you love me because I have attached it as Addendum C. Read it for comprehension, not for memorization. Read it now and several more times between now and when you test. It certainly will not do you any harm!

> B. *Models and promotes the highest standard of conduct, ethical principles, and integrity in decision making, actions, and behaviors.*

Ethics and integrity are displayed in the way you conduct yourself personally and professionally. Actions speak louder than words. Regardless of what kind of lip service is paid to a mantra of all students being able to learn, talk is nothing unless you put what you say into practice on a consistent and daily basis. Trust is so easy to destroy, and equally difficult to regain. It is important to listen to your constituents with a truly open mind rather than to make decisions based on preconceived perceptions. Decisions should be data driven rather than perception driven. It is very hard to repair the damage and credibility among school staff if they think you have made a decision based on bias, partiality, or just plain stubbornness. Constituents need to know and understand why decisions are made. As long as reasonably possible, they should be collaborative. People will support what they helped create, or decide. Before taking action, ask yourself if it will pass the smell test. If someone else sees you doing something that you think is perfectly fine, would it smell to them? Would it cause suspicion? Would they think you are getting by with doing something they cannot, or should not, do? If so, this action smells. Remember, something can be totally innocent, but given just the right twist, it can appear unethical. Be cautious. Always act with discretion. Err on the side of caution. Someone is always watching and listening, and, often, more than likely to repeat whatever it is you said or did. Continuous modeling and promoting "the highest standard of conduct, ethical principles, and integrity in decision making, actions, and behaviors" may sound like common sense. Unfortunately, too often there is an uncommon lack of common sense. Be careful. Be prudent. As shown in Figure 15.1, always measure everything you do by your moral compass. You have one. Use it.

FIGURE 15.1   Competency-Based Principals Have a Moral Compass

Competency-Based Principals

- Act With Integrity
- Act Fairly
- Act Ethically
- Act Legally
- Act Equitably
- Honor Diversity

Verlie Edwards

C. *Advocates for all children by promoting the continuous and appropriate development of all learners in the campus community.*

The key words here are "continuous" and "appropriate." Students are going to develop regardless. They may, or may not, develop in appropriate ways. It is the responsibility of the principal, as well as all society, to see to it that all students have continuous and appropriate development. *Continuous* means all the time, without ceasing. It means you can never give up on seeking to mentor and guide the development of every student with whom you have contact. It is not limited to academic achievement but to every facet of student maturation. For those who think they did not enter education to take on raising every single child, there is one thing to remember: The role of educators *is* to nurture every student continuously.

D. *Implements strategies to ensure that all students have access to effective educators and continuous opportunities to learn.*

It is the responsibility of the principal to ensure all teachers are at the top of their game. If they are not, it is their students who are hurt. Every student deserves their teacher's full attention, skill, and full assurance that they are being given every imaginable opportunity to learn in both traditional and with new research-based strategies.

E. *Promotes awareness and appreciation of diversity throughout the campus community (e.g., learning differences, multicultural awareness, gender sensitivity, and ethnic appreciation).*

All people, whether they are three years old or fifty years old, learn differently. This isn't news. Yet for many classrooms in the United States, teachers act as if they did not realize that learning is a part of our diversified society. They continue to stand and deliver instruction that often is not one bit meaningful to the experiences, culture, race, gender, or ethnicity of students who are held captives in the classroom sitting there not really listening or caring. And then we wonder about the future of education.

If we know the diversity of our students includes having different learning styles and modalities, that they come with different socio-economics, experiences, genders, and cultures, why are we treating them as if we think every one of them is alike? As positive, proactive, student-centered school leaders, it is imperative that we promote awareness of learning differences, multicultural awareness, gender sensitivity, as well as ethnic and religious appreciation. Promoting it by articulation only is not enough. You must be proactively role modeling the type of leadership you expect teachers and others to display in classrooms and the community. Furthermore, you must reward appropriate behavior from your staff members. Praise them. Nurture a vision for the school that includes and appreciates every student, teacher, and community member regardless of their differences.

> F. *Facilitates and supports special campus programs that provide all students with quality, flexible instructional programs and services (e.g., health, guidance, and counseling programs) to meet individual student needs.*

Remember that "facilitate" is one of the test developers' favorite Sherrys. Whenever you see it, pay particular attention. To facilitate something means you may, or may not, actually be the person doing something. Usually it is a committee or the Site-Based Decision-Making Team. Your role is to facilitate their needs, not necessarily to do the work yourself single-handedly.

In this instance, you are facilitating and supporting special campus programs that provide all—not just the easy to teach—students quality, flexible instructional programs and services (e.g., health, guidance, and counseling programs) to meet their individual student needs. This is a big one, folks, so pay close attention to it. The key words are *quality* and *flexible*. Just because a child is in fourth grade does not always mean they are reading on fourth-grade level. The same is true for all content areas.

So what are you supposed to do?

Work with teachers to make sure they have the resources they need to individually teach each child on their own level and bring their learning voids up as much as possible.

> G. *Applies legal guidelines (e.g., in relation to students with disabilities, bilingual education, confidentiality, and discrimination) to protect the rights of students and staff and to improve learning opportunities.*

Two vital responsibilities of any principal are to protect the rights of students and staff members and to improve learning opportunities. It shouldn't be necessary to be reminded of legal guidelines. Individual educational plans (IEPs) provide a good example of the need to apply legal guidelines. If a student with a disability moves to your school and his IEP says he should jump rope backward in the shade of a west-facing tree at 10:01 every morning, you had better make sure he does just that until another admission, review, and/or dismissal meeting (ARD) can be held to modify his care plan. Until then, it is the law.

Various examples of legal guidelines regarding students with disabilities, bilingual education, confidentiality, and discrimination are provided in the competency that addresses concerns within the school community. An easier way to remember which guidelines to apply is to consistently apply them all. If it is the law or a policy, do it. If you truly hate it, contact your legislator or other policymaker to discuss why you hate it and why you think it should be changed.

This is an area that can get you in trouble real quick. The areas of special education, bilingual education, and English as a second language can be subject to audits. You don't want to be "that school" that gets chosen to audit and come up lacking. Therefore, it is critically important to ensure you are following all *state and federal guidelines.* You will not be left alone to die on the stake by yourself. Each district has someone who is ultimately responsible for these programs, who knows *all* the rules and regulations, and is there to help you. Utilize their knowledge and support!

Further, never break any confidentiality laws. Unless otherwise cited by a judge, the only people you can discuss a child's progress with are his or her parents or legal guardian. Be very careful about this.

Last, remember that special programs are any programs that enhance students' learning. These obviously include counseling, health, and guidance programs, but also include all forms of academic support, particularly for students with learning disabilities.

In short, you must consistently apply all legal guidelines (e.g., in relation to students with disabilities, bilingual education, confidentiality, and discrimination) to protect the rights of students and staff and to improve learning opportunities.

H. Articulates the importance of education in a free, democratic society.

To articulate is to communicate the importance of education to everyone, everywhere. It is the role of all educators, not just administrators, to articulate the importance of education in a free democratic society. If it's not our responsibility, then whose is it? It has been said that today's principals are so busy with trivia and management duties, there's little time left for the role of statesperson that educators traditionally have played. We cannot let this responsibility slip away. It is one we carry with us at school, at home, at church, in the community, and in everything we do.

PRIORITIZED STATEMENTS

C. *Advocates for all children by promoting the continuous and appropriate development of all learners in the campus community.*

D. *Implements strategies to ensure that all students have access to effective educators and continuous opportunities to learn.*

E. *Promotes awareness and appreciation of diversity throughout the campus community (e.g., learning differences, multicultural awareness, gender sensitivity, and ethnic appreciation).*

F. *Facilitates and supports special campus programs that provide all students with quality, flexible instructional programs and services (e.g., health, guidance, and counseling programs) to meet individual student needs.*

G. *Applies legal guidelines (e.g., in relation to students with disabilities, bilingual education, confidentiality, and discrimination) to protect the rights of students and staff and to improve learning opportunities.*

IMPORTANT POINTS TO REMEMBER

- Make sure your walk matches your talk.

- Be the Ideal Principal.

- Be a good, open-minded listener.

- All decisions should be data based.

- All students do not learn at the same rate or time. Accommodate accordingly.

- Diversity in learning covers more than race.

- Facilitate everything.

- Always stay legal.

- Be the best spokesperson for a free and appropriate public education that the world has ever seen.

SECTION III

The Real Deal

Practical Application

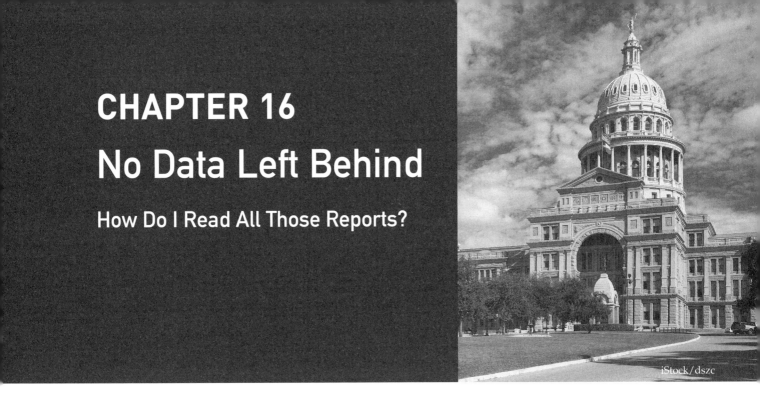

CHAPTER 16
No Data Left Behind
How Do I Read All Those Reports?

iStock/dszc

DATA ANALYSIS SIMPLIFIED

Being able to analyze data is critical to your success as a principal and in passing either of the administrative TExES exams (principal or superintendent). Yet data analysis remains one of the things that scares test takers the most. It should not. There are some basic tools to utilize that will help you get a profile of the data. Remember, the TExES exam is built around knowledge and skills that an *entry-level* principal should have. You do not need to know how to disaggregate data for a multivariate statistical doctoral dissertation to pass this test.

HOW TO READ AND INTERPRET STANDARDIZED TEST SCORES

There is no guarantee that you will have a decision set, or any other data to analyze and apply, that is built on standardized tests, their results, or their implications. However, there is also no guarantee that you will *not*. Some people make a big mistake. They turn a page in their test booklet, see all those graphs, and think, "Here come those awful Texas Academic Performance Report (TAPR) Reports," or "Oh, dear. I really hate disaggregating State of Texas Assessments of Academic Readiness (STAAR) test scores," or "I am an elementary person. What's with all these high school End-of-Course (EOC) test scores?" These people's first response is to panic.

Panicking is not good. As previously shown in Figure 1.2, when anxiety goes up, productivity goes down.

So you are not going to panic. You do not want your productivity to go down. After all, how can you be calm, cool, collected, confident, and almost downright cocky if you are panicking? So do not panic. Take a deep breath, blow it out slowly, and do what I tell you to do.

Read the prompt for the decision set or data analysis slowly for comprehension purposes. Ascertain what it is really trying to tell you. The prompt will lay the groundwork of what the upcoming questions will be about. It will give you the feel of what the test developers are looking for. There is never anything to frighten you in the prompt. All the prompt does is tell you the direction you are going. So read it and see what you are dealing with. Write down key words or phrases on your scratch paper, which will be provided. Get the feel of the school you will be analyzing from the way it is described in the prompt.

Once you have done that, look at the charts or graphs provided. Think big picture. At this point, you are *only* interested in the big picture. Standardized tests in these scenarios are usually STAAR, EOC, or TAPR reports/tests. Achievement tests, in various forms, have been around longer than any of our Texas high-stakes tests and are something virtually every campus in the nation either is dealing with or has dealt with. You need to know how to analyze, interpret, and utilize them to increase student performance. These data provide the parameters to tell you where your school's, as well as each student's, strengths and weaknesses lie. They are crucial for strategic short- and long-term planning.

Look at each chart or graph individually. What is this exact set of data about? What subject is the data referring to? Identify both. Keep breathing slowly, deeply, and confidently. Frankly, you do not *care* what grade or subject the data is about or whether it is elementary or secondary, other than to be prepared for whatever questions may, or may not, be coming your way. Do not think, "Oh, my goodness! These are math scores! I hate math, and I doubly hate math scores!" Do not go there. It will not make one bit of difference if the scores are math, reading, science, or anything else. Scores are scores. The real question is what are you going to do with them? How are you going to lead and facilitate others to use this data to make informed decisions, also known as *data-driven decision making*, which will impact the campus vision, curriculum, and instruction? These are the important issues that the TExES exam will want to know that you know how to do. They want to know that you can read the data and that you can analyze it for use in improving student learning. Period. It is all about improving student learning. Nothing else matters. Helping students learn, using every resource possible is what matters.

Next, if you have a chart, look across the top and down the left side to see what your headings are. The headings provide you with the categories of content that have been tested as well as the rating scales used. Read the concepts the students have been tested on. They likely will be grouped in broad categories. This provides you the basic overview of what was tested. This helps constitute the big picture that you want to have before you start to read the questions within each decision set. Look next at the rating scales to see how they are categorized.

At this point, you can make some obvious conclusions ranging from, "This grade, content area, or campus did pretty well," to "This is horrible. The students do not appear to be learning much of anything. I need to be in charge of this school to turn it around!" You may notice some particular areas where the grade, content area, or campus did very well, or some areas where they did particularly bad—which is a polite way of saying they stunk. More likely, the majority of their scores will be somewhere in between.

This is important. As shown in Figure 16.1, high scores, or scores that are moving upward, are *campus strengths.* Low scores, or scores that are moving downward, are *campus weaknesses.* High scores are good. Low scores are bad. Every school has both strengths and weaknesses. However, one school's weakness may be another school's strength. You are interested in

- On the day of the test, the school presented in the decision set

- In the future, the school where you are the ideal principal moving your campus from reality toward ideal

FIGURE 16.1   Identifying Campus Strengths, Weaknesses, and Trends

Low Scores ——————————→ Areas of Weakness

High Scores ——————————→ Areas of Strength

Moving Scores ——————————→ Potential Trends

Leanne Ivey

Having said that, this is a high-stakes test for you so, sometimes, your nervous instinct will be to play the "What If? Game." Nowhere in this book do I tell you to try to second guess what the test developers may ask you. Nowhere do I tell you to play the "What if? Game." Do not try to be psychic with the potentially mass of data by thinking, "What if they ask me something I don't know? What else can I conclude from these data? What *could* they ask me? Oh, my goodness. I do not even know what these concepts stand for! What if they ask me something I am clueless about?" While you are, thus, playing the "What If? Game," two things are happening:

- Your anxiety level is going up. We all know by now what happens when your anxiety level goes up. We do not want that. Definitely not! We do not want your anxiety level so low, as evidenced by regular huge sighs, that people around you think you are on Prozac. Leave the "What If? Game" alone. I give you plenty of *productive* techniques. Right now, just identify the broad categories the data represent, and move on. Do *not* try to read the minds of the test developers regarding what they may ask. After all, they got paid for developing the test. You did not. Your job is to pass the test.

- The clock is ticking. You have plenty of time to take and pass this test. However, it makes no sense to waste the time you have. There is no reason for you to sit there, staring at all that data while playing the "What If? Game." You do not want to *wonder*. You want to *know*. Thus, while you are wondering what they *might* ask you, the clock is ticking away your precious minutes. No, no, no! You are not going there. Turn the page. Go see what they *are* asking rather than fretting over *What If?* It is a better utilization of your limited time, keeps you on track and focused, and keeps you working *with* the clock rather than against it.

Remember, in your initial view of the data, all you want to do is get the essence of what it is presenting, such as grade, subject, basic concepts tested, and an overview of how the grade, content area, or campus performed.

Next, turn the page, and get started on the actual questions. This test is a mind game. Do not let it psych you out. Beat it at its own game. Stay confident. Keep taking those slow, deep, steady breaths. Keep reading, answering, and turning those pages.

The Pleasant Surprise

Here is the *pleasant* surprise. In an entire decision set, rarely do they ask more than two to three questions that will actually require you to *look* at the data. The rest of the questions will be generic in nature, similar to questions in any other decision set. But if you are hyped up over what they *might* ask you, you could miss the basic questions. That is the surprise benefit of not getting yourself worked up or playing the "What If? Game." Just go see what they really *are* asking. This keeps your anxiety down, your productivity up, and the clock as your friend instead of your enemy.

When you do come to the questions that actually have you look at the data, you do not have to be a statistical whiz. They are looking for *entry-level* data analysis knowledge and skills. Therefore, if they ask you where a large or the larg*est* need in the campus, grade, or content area is, look for the *lowest* scores or those on a downward trend. Low scores indicate need for improvement. As shown in Figure 16.1, downward trends indicate we are going the wrong direction and require immediate intervention to turn the situation around.

Even the best campus has a low area in *something.* Until *every* student at every school has 100% mastery of *every* concept on every test, there is always a need to improve. Having 100% mastery means all students are learning. This includes students with various disabilities as well as language, economic, and cultural differences. It represents an ideal situation. Remember, the ideal principal is all about *every* student doing well and the campus being on a constant move toward becoming ideal. Doing this is a classic example of being a reflective and data-sensitive leader. Every principal, teacher, and member of the campus community must continuously ask themselves and others, "How can we do *everything* better?" This is called using data for reflection and for continuous student learning improvement. It makes no difference if we are discussing math scores, band competitions, or the Pillsbury Bake-Off. Until every student masters every objective, we are not there yet. We are not through seeking improvement. We do not have time to rest on our laurels and think as Scarlet O'Hara did, "I'll think about it tomorrow at Tara." We must lead our schools *today* to prepare educated, informed, and productive citizens necessary for the American democratic society of tomorrow.

However, we cannot wait until tomorrow to think about the difficult tasks ahead of us. We cannot procrastinate. We must always and forever be asking, "How can we do this better?" Identify it, and do it. There are no excuses. Excuses are for losers. *You* will lead your students, faculty, and other stakeholders to know that they are *winners.* There is no time to waste. To enhance student performance as measured by standardized test scores, you must know how to read, analyze, draw conclusions about, and facilitate the implementation and assessment of programs, curriculum, instructional strategies, and personnel that will meet the needs of today's students on your campus. Do not focus unduly on what is working elsewhere. That is not your job. Your job is to create the best organizational culture and climate to facilitate maximized student performance on your campus. As shown in Figure 16.1, the answers to where the areas are to address are in the data. Every school has different strengths and weaknesses. Your role is to know your data inside out, to be able to speak fluently and coherently about them to anyone who will listen, and to always be thinking of new and better ways to engage and enhance student learning.

Therefore, refer back to Figure 16.1 yet again. If a question steers you toward areas of *growth* within a campus, grade, or content area, you will look at the numbers to see the greatest difference in a *positive*, not a negative, direction. If a question asks you where the schools greatest strengths are, look for the *bigger numbers* or the areas showing the *greatest upward trends.* It could be that one category of concepts or a certain grade is still higher than another, *but* those scores are stagnant or even regressing a tiny bit. At the same time, another area may be showing consistent, steady, albeit slow, growth. If the numbers are consistently coming up, even if it is slowly, that is a positive thing and should be noticed, praised, and supplemented. Watch for answers that catch trends like that. The test developers love to throw in responses that determine if you are utilizing higher-order thinking skills by catching trends or implications. Show them you are by selecting the correct response.

You will not be asked any detailed or advanced statistical analysis questions. That is not the primary role of the principal and certainly not a beginning principal. The test does not ask you about variances or standard deviations, so relax. They do want to know that you know how to determine if students in your campus are learning, what their individual and collective strengths and weaknesses are, and that you are leading planning processes to increase student performance for *all* students based on the evidence of scores presented. If students from *all* subgroups are not learning, why aren't they? What can be done to improve the culture, climate, instruction, and curriculum of the campus such that *all* students can and do learn? Therefore, the purpose of any testing is threefold. The purposes are to

- measure student growth;

- assess student and campus strengths, weaknesses, and trends; and

- use data as a valid means of determining goals for student growth and improvement for the campus, grade, subgroups, and content areas.

Last, remember, it does not matter how high the preponderance of your students' scores are, if *everyone* is not learning. This test is about *all* students, not just some of them. Ideal principals never, ever, ever give up until *every* student is mastering every concept. *You* are striving to become an ideal principal. Campus excellence is not determined simply by the scores of students who are motivated and easy to teach. Campus excellence is determined by the success of *all* students in *all* areas. Excellence is for *everyone.* Do you think this philosophy is unrealistic? Fine. It may be. But we do not care about realistic. We care about ideal. There are other jobs available for those who lose sight of the ideal. Places outside education are hiring. There are plenty of jobs for those who only want a paycheck and do not have a passion for excellence in learning for everyone to further the promulgation of an enhanced American democratic society. As for you, you are on your own quest for educational excellence. If you are not on this quest, as your campus prepares for the test, *pretend* you are! This test is about excellence for all. *If you do not truly believe this can be attained, you will not pass this test.* If you do believe all students can and will learn provided they have the right curriculum, differentiated instruction, resources, and support services, you are on your way to being a cutting-edge, highly effective principal.

HOW TO READ AND INTERPRET A "TEXAS ACADEMIC PERFORMANCE REPORT" (TAPR)

Whereas students all across America in both public and private schools take achievement tests, the TAPR is exclusive to Texas. Every district and campus is rated by this important accountability system based largely on data detailed in the annual TAPR report. Two important areas are student passing rates on the STAAR and EOC exams and student attendance. These have no impact on how you answer questions since each of the tests is built around increasing student performance for all students.

As you begin looking at any TAPR report, and as provided in Addendum B, first look at the overall report to see what you have been given. There are *three specific areas* to consider. You may or may not be given each of these areas to analyze, but you want to know about them all, just in case. First is the cover or title page. It tells you the academic year of testing, as well as the name, campus number, and state rating of the overall campus.

The subsequent TAPR report is one long report as shown in Addendum B. It is no longer divided into Section I and Section II. It just starts and keeps on going. Still has the same framework, but it is now rolled into one long report with no dividing sections. There are certain things that always appear and never change. Memorize them. Please notice this is the first time I have asked you to memorize anything. I did not ask you to memorize any of the eleven competencies. I asked you to fully understand and comprehend them so you would recognize what the test developers are questioning you about. Yet now I am asking you to memorize the order of the categories of the TAPR as shown in Figure 16.2. Doing this will save time and anxiety in searching through a report to find the data you need to make informed responses to your test questions.

Therefore, when determining where to look for an appropriate answer, if the question has anything to do with test scores or student attendance, you know the answer will be in the front of the TAPR. You can, thus, ignore the rest of the data.

FIGURE 16.2 Components of a TAPR Report

1. Test Data
2. Attendance
3. Student Information (except testing)
4. Staff Information

5. Actual Operating Expenditure Information
6. Budget Information
7. Program Information

Michael Whitney

For ease in navigating the report, the section and page numbers are listed in the top right corner of each page. Now, let's look deeper into what these things mean.

Student Testing Data

As shown at the beginning, any TAPR report addresses everything you would ever want to know, or not want to know, about student performance. It is presented in a chart format. STAAR, and formerly TAKS, begins in the third grade and continues through Grade 8. It was originally given primarily in reading, math, and writing with secondary schools also reporting EOC test results. Subsequently, tests in both science and social studies were added. Some subjects, such as writing, science, and social studies, are not given in every grade; thus, there will not be any scores reported for the grades in which they are not given. Currently, STAAR is not given on the secondary level. Secondary EOC exams are given in twelve areas. These are English I, English II, English III, Algebra I, Algebra II, Geography, World Geography, World History, U.S. History, Biology, Chemistry, and Physics. Test results are reported at the very beginning of TAPR regardless if it is an elementary or secondary school.

Also shown in Addendum A, the student groups are listed at the top of the chart from left to right with the largest subgroup coming first and going in decreasing size to the various demographic subgroups. For the sake of our discussion, let's say that we are presented with a TAPR report that is looking at third-grade reading and math scores. Writing is not given in the third grade so it, obviously, is not shown. It is helpful to think "big to little" in looking at each subgroup and how it performed. Individual student scores are never known on either a campus or campus TAPR report. Individual student performance is provided on the campus level and protected by privacy laws. In other words, while you may go online to see how any campus or district in Texas did on their TAPR report, you cannot determine how Little Johnny Next Door did on his tests. It is not there. If you are asked any question that seeks to check your knowledge of student privacy and confidentiality, the answer is the public does *not* get to see or access individual student records.

The biggest group is the *State*, so state results appear in the first column. Under this column, the scores of students per grade and subject are provided. In our example of third grade, the column shows how all third graders in Texas did on reading and math. Everyone, and especially the press, wants to compare and contrast how your campus did in comparison to the overall state. No one wants to be below the state average in any area.

Each year, detailed demographic data about every student in every campus as well as data about the campus itself is entered by staff (not you, thank goodness) into the Big State Computer in the Clouds otherwise called the Public Education Information Management System (PEIMS). The Big State Computer in the Clouds crunches all the numbers and codes for various factors such as race, gender, student age, grade, socioeconomics, mobility, campus wealth, and so forth. Each campus is subsequently given an opportunity to correct erroneous information at specific points during the year to assure data accuracy. As a principal, it is in your best interest for this information to be perfect.

You may wonder why having accurate PEIMS data is so important. Let me explain it to you. Let's say that you are principal of Poor Me Middle School. Poor Me Middle School is, gee, rather pitiful. For example, 100% of the students are eligible for free or reduced-price lunch. No one speaks English. No one lives in a single-family dwelling. In fact, virtually everyone lives in low-rent property and moves all the time. Thus, students at your school are constantly changing and rarely get to establish many roots. Few of the homes have two parents in them. Unemployment, alcohol, and drugs abound. For the sake of discussion, I am overexaggerating, but you get the point. Poor Me Middle School has had dismal scores on all forms of student testing for years and has earned sympathy from everyone because, gee, they are a rather pitiful lot. Who could expect them to perform very well academically? They have been pitiful and gotten by with it without too much protest. Poor Me Middle School is your classic example of low expectations and reaping what you sow. If you do not think a student or campus will produce much, guess what: They won't. Fortunately, the opposite is also true. If we know that to be true, why do we not expect high performance out of everyone?

Now that you have done such a good job improving student performance as principal of Poor Me MS, you have been solicited to apply, and ultimately get, the principal position at Pretty Good High School. Pretty Good High School is in the same geographic area as Poor Me Independent School District, but that is all they have in common. At Pretty Good Independent School District, there is no rental property. Everyone owns their home and is proud of it. Everyone speaks English and maybe another couple of languages just for fun. No one qualifies for free or reduced-price lunch. There is virtually no mobility. In fact, parents of kindergarteners are already requesting the teachers they want their children to have in first, second, or third grade! Almost every home has two parents plus maybe a maid or a nanny. No one rides the bus because children walk or ride their bikes safely to school, or neighborhood car pools pick them up to take them to scouts, soccer practice, gymnastics, or piano lessons. Along the way, they stop and have a snow cone or ice cream. Life is so nice at Pretty Good High School. Not surprisingly, so are the test scores. They are pretty good.

But they are not *excellent*. Administrators, faculty, staff, and even the school board members at Pretty Good Independent School District have been content with the high school campus's pretty good scores. After all, they *always* outperform those poor, pitiful little children over at Poor Me Independent School District, God bless them. Here at Pretty Good Independent School District, students can do relatively well without too much extra effort. They look pretty good under the *State* and *District* columns, so what is the problem?

That is where the *Campus* comes in handy. Now scores from Pretty Good High School are being compared to scores from other pretty good high schools across the state. Oops! What principal would like to explain to the superintendent, school board, and community why, although their scores are pretty good, they are *below* the *District or State*? This would not be a happy conversation. Therefore, instruction at all the Pretty Good campuses also becomes much more focused and data driven. The result is improved curriculum, instruction, and assessment in the Pretty Good, Poor Me, and all other campuses in the state. Although some consider the *Campus* a headache, it actually is a good thing. It keeps all schools on their toes and cognizant of how other schools are doing. The net results are improved learning and accountability for everyone. In simple language, the *Campus* holds us all accountable for teaching and learning every day. If a principal is not leading and facilitating improved student learning for truly altruistic reasons, the TAPR report should take care of it.

The *Campus* column is not the first column in the "big to little" sequence, it is the first column you look at because, honey, it is *your campus*. State law now requires student performance scores from the campus TAPR report to be used in the principal's annual evaluation. Believe me, the scores presented here are of the utmost importance to your job security. To facilitate easy reading, highlight your scores in yellow as soon as you receive your TAPR. Study, and think about them virtually 24 hours a day. These data should be critical elements in guiding all subsequent analysis and discussion of campus needs and goal setting. How will you lead your campus personnel, as well as the community, to improve student performance based on these and campus-level data? What are other important sources of data that should be included in campus strategic planning?

After the *Campus* column, still thinking "big to little," the columns are divided into various student subgroups. These include African American, Hispanic, White, American Indian, Asian/Pacific Islanders, Male, Female, Economically Disadvantaged, and Special Education. The goal is for every subgroup to do well, including Special Education. You do not want to see any large differences in passing rates of students on any section of any test. If you do, you and your stakeholders must ask why *all* your students are not performing well. Then create plans and strategies to resolve the discrepancies. In the ideal campus, instruction is individualized and curriculum is developmentally appropriate such that there will be no significant deviations between subgroups. When, in reality, there are deviations, intense study and planning are undertaken by many stakeholders to resolve the situation such that all students learn with maximized performance for their varying ability levels. This is not simply an idealistic philosophy. It is reality in today's schools.

Those are all the categories placed into columns. Along the left side of each page in the first portion of the test are rows labeled with the subjects tested such as reading, math, writing, science, social studies, or *All Tests*. Appropriate scores are noted on two lines for the current year and the previous year. In each area, you will want your scores to be coming *up* annually, not going down. If they are going down or remaining stagnant, again, you and your campus community must analyze *why* and plan for both short- and long-term improvement.

The *All Tests* is an interesting row. It is there to determine the percentage of students who passed every test they took. It is necessary, because if you just looked at the individual subjects and compared results, you would get a less than complete picture. For example, let's go back to our hypothetical set of campus third-grade scores. Say 50% of the third graders passed reading, and 50% of the third graders passed math. At first glance, you might think, "Well, 50% of the students in third grade are doing really well. The other 50% cannot read or do math."

This could be a wrong conclusion. What if it was a *different* set of students who passed each portion?

- What if 50% of them actually have the ability to read *War and Peace* but could not successfully add 2 + 2?

- What if the other 50% could work algorithms but could not read *The Cat in the Hat*?

Hmm. We have a problem here. This problem is why we have the *All Tests* row. It allows us to see an overall picture of exactly what percentage of the campus is passing *everything* taken. The goal is to have 100% of the students passing all tests.

The first portion of all TAPR reports is always set up in this format. Therefore, this is where you would look if you were asked any questions that relate to specific grade-level or subgroup performance on any test for any grade or for the campus as a whole. If you are asked to compare scores, ascertain trends, or identify strengths or weaknesses of performance, this is also where you would look.

The next portion is a summary of all the scores in the campus. The rows and columns of the chart remain the same. It says *STARR % Passing Sum of 3–8 & 10.* If the campus you are analyzing is quite small and does not have all those grades, it does not matter. This chart is simply a quick reference guide to the overall performance of how the entire campus did on the specified subjects and *All Tests*. If you are asked any questions about overall campus performance, this is where you would look first.

Continuing, you will see a large variety of comparisons of various student groups. This is important because although it will be wonderful if you have 100% passing rates in every category above, if you have exempted half the campus, it is not a good reason why. Superintendents, school boards, as well as the state itself, look at this closely. They do not want you exempting high percentages of students. Their goal is for everyone to test and score well. Therefore, this section shows the percentage of students, per subgroup, that you have exempted for any reason, including special education or Limited English Proficiency (LEP) purposes. Again, it is *very important* for you to have low percentages in this area. Special education students must now test in alternative ways, and scores are reported. *Exemptions* are one of the few places that you want your numbers to be *less* than the *State, Campus*, or *District*. You particularly do *not* want high percentages of exemptions or bad scores within any of your subgroups. Again, the goal is for everyone to test and everyone to do well. We want *all* students to learn and learn well, even if they are difficult to teach.

Student Attendance

Attendance is important because if students are not coming to school, it is difficult for them to maximize their learning opportunities, or at least the things you want them to learn. The same format for grouping columns previously described is also used here. The important thing to notice is that the 2 years listed are always 1 year behind. That is not an accident, nor is it placed there to confuse you. The reason is simple. This academic year is not over yet; therefore, it is impossible to determine the total percentage of attendance. Obviously, you want your attendance percentages to be *higher* than your *State* or *District*. You do want to see high attendance percentage rates among all campus subgroups. If a certain subgroup has low attendance, it is critically important to ascertain *why.* Why are these students not coming to school? What can we as a campus or community do to address this situation? Again, if students are not in attendance, it is going to be very difficult for them to learn. Also, since this is Texas, and we have a rule or regulation for everything, if attendance becomes too low or dropout rates become too high, the campus will be cited by the State with very serious consequences. These consequences, if not addressed, could result in the campus receiving bad ratings, being put under a state "master" for leadership, or ultimately being closed. Needless to say, these are not things any campus wants to have happen. A major goal of a democratic society is to produce literate, cognizant, contributing citizens. This is hard to do when students are not in school.

Student Information

The *Student Information* section is still presented in chart format. The subgroups no longer appear. The basic layout is *Campus, District,* and *State.* You will be given basic student enrollment (*not testing*) information such as how many students and what percentage of your enrollment is in each grade of the campus. It is further disaggregated into *Ethnic Distribution, Mobility, Economically Disadvantaged, Limited English Proficient, Number of Students per Teacher,* and *Retention Rates.* This is charted in rows comparing this campus to their *District* and the *State.* Other than *Number of Students per Teacher* and *Retention Rates by Grade* for both regular and special education students, there is no doing better or worse than these groups. These are merely facts. However, you would like to see a small ratio of students to teachers as well as a *small* percentage of student retention. Although this section does not relate to testing, it is an important place to look when you are analyzing a report. Just as you do not want high passing rates due to high exemption rates, you also do not want high passing rates due to flunking everyone. This is the kind of critical thinking that test developers like to see if you will catch. Watch for it. We want everyone doing well on STAAR and EOCs, of course, but *not* because the campus exempted or flunked everyone at risk of not passing the test. Basically though, if you are given a question that pertains to *Enrollment, Ethnic Distribution, Mobility, Economically Disadvantaged, Limited English Proficiency, Number of Students per Teacher,* or *Retention Rates by Grade* for either regular or special education students, then the *Student Information* chart is where you would look. Remember this is where to find it for test-taking day.

Staff Information

The next section is *Staff Information.* It is set up in the same *Count, Percent, District,* and *State* format as *Student Information.* This is where you will look to determine numbers and percentages of staff who are *Professional* (teachers, professional support, and campus administration), plus *Educational Aides, Total Staff, Total Minority Staff, Teachers by Ethnicity and*

Sex, Teachers by Years of Experience, Average Years of Experience of Teachers, Average Years of Experience of Teachers with Campus, Average Teacher Salary by Years of Experience, and *Average Actual Salaries* for teachers, professional support, and campus administration. These data are public information and freely available to any citizen who wants to see them either by hard copy or via the Internet. The TAPR report brings various data together in one report.

If you are asked any questions regarding average salaries for virtually anyone, this is where you would look. If you were asked questions that involve planning for future personnel needs, one place to look would be at the average years of experience of campus staff to begin thinking about future retirements and their potential effect on staffing, the budget, and instruction. This is where you would look to see how well your campus is doing in comparison to the others in recruiting and retaining minority staff. This is a pressing issue for all schools. Because this is such a common issue statewide, watch for it as a common theme that could appear on the test.

For virtually any question you may have that relates to staffing, the *Staff Information* segment is where you would look first. Always think, "Is there any place else I could look for something that could be of importance to answering this, or any, question?" Remember, the competencies refer to using multiple sources of data repeatedly. By becoming familiar with exactly where to find what you're looking for in the TAPR report, you can utilize multiple pieces of information from within the same document to make an intelligent, data-driven decision.

Actual Operating Expenditure Information

The next component is *Actual Operating Expenditure Information*. This is where you will find everything about the budget in a summarized form. The format again compares the *Campus* and *State*. A rule of thumb is that principals, superintendents, school boards, and especially taxpayers like test scores to be *higher* than anyone else's, but for the campus to be doing it with *less* money. Using that rationale, this plus student retention and the teacher-student ratio are the places you would like your numbers to be *less* than your comparison groups. The first place was in Section I in *Exempted Sum of 3–8*. We discussed it again in *Number of Students per Teacher* and *Retention Rates by Grade*. When it comes to money, always look for financial *prudence*. This is particularly true in relation to administrative costs. Boards and taxpayers like to see money targeted directly toward students and instruction and as little as possible toward administration. Within the *Actual Operating Expenditure Information* you will find the actual amount and percentage of the budget for the *Total Campus Budget* by *Function* and *Per Pupil*. Think, "Scores up, costs down." Remember this when looking at both budgets and test results. Remember this especially on the day you take your TExES exam.

Program Information

The last chart is *Program Information.* This is where you will find how many students are in each category of the campus program as well as the amount of money spent on each. *Program Information* uses the consistent Section II chart format of columns for *Count, Percent, District, Campus,* and *State.* The rows then provide the categories. These are *Student Enrollment by Program* for *Special Education, Career & Technology Education, Bilingual/ ESL Education,* and *Gifted & Talented Education.* It provides the numbers and percentages of *Teachers by Program* for *Regular, Special, Compensatory, Career & Technology, Bilingual/ESL, Gifted & Talented,* and *Other.* Next, it details the *Budgeted Instructional Operating Expenditures by Program* for each. If you are asked questions about program equity, particularly in the area of finance, this would be where you would first look.

My last suggestion for you in data analysis is to utilize your common sense. Think prudently. Improving student performance is your guiding principle in every instance. That is what they are looking for, so show it to them in your answer choices.

Similar to standardized test results, you will look at the overview of what you have been given. The top right corner of every page will provide this information. By referring to Figure 16.2 you can easily remember what types of information can be found at the beginning, middle, and end of a TAPR report. Go directly to the questions to see exactly what they are asking rather than playing the "What If? Game" of what they *might* ask. This saves time, effort, and anxiety.

SUMMARY

In closing our study of data analysis through standardized tests and TAPR reports, remember to do these things:

- Look to see the profile of what you have been given. What kind of test or what portion of a TAPR report has been provided for your review?

- What concepts or components are made available?

- Do *not* play the "What If? Game." Do *not* try to be psychic by trying to draw conclusions about the data *before* you read each question. Turn the page, and *read* the questions. Then you will know where to look and what to analyze per question.

- The test is looking only for *entry-level* data analysis skills. Keep your anxiety level down so your productivity will stay *up.*

- Practice looking at various standardized test results and TAPR reports within your own campus or on the Internet before the TExES exam so that you will be familiar and comfortable with forms and layout.

- Memorize the order information is presented in a TAPR report. This will save you time and anxiety on the day you test because you will know exactly where to look for the answers.

Knowing and becoming familiar with the *format* of a TAPR report, plus knowing the order things always come in, turns a scary and sometimes formidable portion of the TExES exam into a very workable passage. Knowing this and making yourself familiar with multiple TAPR reports from various campuses before the test will help you walk into your test *cool, calm, collected, confident, and almost downright cocky.* This confidence level is what you want as you *ace* this test.

CHAPTER 17

Test-Taking Strategies

Now Listen to Me Here . . .

iStock/dszc

Without continual growth and progress, such words as improvement, achievement, and success have no meaning.

—Benjamin Franklin

It is assumed that students who are preparing for the principal TExES examination have had an appropriate university or alternative preparation program in school leadership. The goal of this book is to enhance that foundation and to help you pass the TExES examination. The purpose is not to reteach your master's degree or certification program. Therefore, assuming you have the prerequisite knowledge base necessary *and* you utilize the philosophy and skills presented in this book, you should *ace* this test. That means you should be able to walk in to take the TExES exam cool, calm, collected, confident, and almost downright cocky. Anxiety is not your friend. As shown earlier in Figure 1.1, when your anxiety goes up, your productivity goes down. The reverse is also true.

The test, from this point on, is a mind game. You have the knowledge and conceptual framework to knock the top out of this test. Therefore, what you think you will achieve, you will achieve. If you think you will pass the test, you will. If you think you will not, you won't. Either way, you will be right. Your mind is the front wheel of the wheelbarrow that leads your life. Go forward with a positive mind-set. Here are strategies to help you.

THE TESTING SESSION: GENERAL OVERVIEW

Organizational guru Stephen Covey (1990) reminds us to sharpen the saw before we begin virtually anything. In this instance, the time you spend studying, analyzing, sorting, and organizing your data is sharpening your saw. It will be time very well spent before you begin answering the test questions. If you do not spend this time effectively and efficiently, you will lose productivity during the remainder of the session, because you have to go back and read the question again to find what is needed to answer the questions appropriately. If you keep these things in mind, once you begin addressing the questions, you will have the big picture of the school already in your mind. Reading a question well, for comprehension of what they are really asking you, is not a waste of time. It is your key to success in picking the best responses. Sharpen your saw well. Remember to always respond to these questions as

- an ideal principal,

- making data-driven and student-focused decisions,

- aligned with the theoretical framework (six domains and eleven competencies),

- using the 1–2–3–4 Plan,

- "The Process" for multiple-multiples, and

- watching for the key concepts, such as the "Sherry List" first shown in Figure 4.2.

Analytical and Problem-Solving Skills

Your exam will consist of multiple-decision sets similar to what you experienced on the Principal Practice TExES exam. Each decision set is composed of a prompt, followed by related questions. When you begin this section, read the prompt that introduces the first decision set. Remember, there are no questions or answers in the prompt. The prompt simply tells you a little bit about the school or situation you will be addressing. As you read, write down key words or kinesthetic concepts on your scrap paper that you think are important. So use your visual senses by writing down key words or important concepts throughout TExES. This will help you stay focused on what the question is really asking and not allow you to become distracted by potentially great responses that do not happen to answer *this* question.

There are specific strategies that will help you. Thus far, you have studied hard for the principal TExES exam. Now it is time to learn other test-taking techniques to help you win this mind game and, subsequently, knock the top off this test.

THE DOT GAME: A PSYCHOLOGICAL AND TIME MANAGEMENT STRATEGY

You will have plenty of time to successfully complete this exam. There is no reason for you to run out of time. However, on rare occasion, I hear of someone who claims they did. I am going to teach you to utilize a deceptively simple technique called The Dot Game. If you play The Dot Game, it is impossible for you to run out of time. Here is how to do it.

After reading the prompt for your first decision set, you will read the first question. You will mark the answer. You will read the next question. You will mark the answer. This will go along just fine until you get to a question where you really are not sure of the answer. This question is one of those that make you go, "Hmmmmm." This happens to everyone, so do not feel bad. Read the question and possible answers again. If you still do not feel confident about which is the correct response, put a dot by the question and move on. Just skip that question. Do not feel guilty. Do not look back. Just put the dot by it on your scrap paper and keep on moving. Don't worry. The Dot Game has steps. You will come back to this question, and any others you leave a dot by, later.

Continue until you hit another question where you are not sure of the answer. Put a dot by it, too. Do not spend over 2 minutes pondering the right answer to any question. The longer you spend trying to figure out the answer, the more your anxiety level will go up. When your anxiety level goes up, your productivity goes down. Worse, the clock is ticking. The clock is not your friend. I am your friend, so listen to me! Put a dot by it, and go on to the next question.

Repeat this process throughout your testing session. I do not care if you have thirty dots when you finish. Big deal. You have accomplished something significant: You have worked your way through the entire test. You know every question and concept they have to throw at you. You've seen it all. The pressure is off.

Here is what I want you to do when you finish going through the test this first time. Close your book. Get up. Go to the restroom. Shake out the tenseness in your muscles. Get a drink of water. Walk around for a minute or two to clear your head and relax. It will be time well spent to rid your body and mind of tension and stress and to loosen up. Then, before you go back in, stop and say out loud to use your auditory sense, "Thank goodness I have made it through this test *the first time*. Now I am going back in there to *finish acing this baby!*" Do not ignore what I am saying. It is important that your subconscious *hear* you affirm that you are going to pass this test. Repeat it over and over, out loud and silently. It is all a part of winning the mind game.

When you go back into the testing room, only return to the questions where you have dots. Remember, when anxiety goes down, productivity goes up. Because of that, you will be pleasantly surprised to see how many questions you will be able to answer quickly this time simply due to four reasons:

1. The pressure is off. You have already seen everything on the test. There is nothing scary left. Psychologically, your subconscious has begun to relax; thus, your productivity will go up.

2. You know that, in this instance, you do not have to make 100 on the TExES exam to pass it. Schools do not really care what your

score is. They only care if you are certified. A passing score on TExES, plus other certification requirements, will accomplish that goal.

3. There is something odd that happens after you have read the entire test. The *philosophy* as well as *key words and phrases* settle into your subconscious and become familiar. If you have *not* spent too long pondering the difficult questions, generally the second time through, the appropriate answers reveal themselves to you quickly. This is not as likely to happen if you have spent too long pondering each question when you read the question initially.

4. You are no longer fighting the clock. You know you have already answered the ones that you are certain of. You do not have to stress over getting through the whole test the first time without running out of time. With this additional pressure off, your mind is freed to better comprehend what the more difficult questions are asking you.

If you do not have all the answers after your second time through, it is perfectly all right. Repeat the process. Close your book. Take a break, just like you did before. Your anxiety level should be *way* down by now because you know that you do not need to make 100. Just passing will do.

Regardless, keep repeating The Dot Game until you have answered all the questions. If that is over three times, guess on the ones you are not sure of and go home. This test is not the GRE. You are not penalized for wrong answers. It is unlikely you will have a divine intervention to tell you the right answers at this point. There is no sense in sitting there forever pondering a question that you are clueless about. Move on.

If you use The Dot Game, there is no way that you can run out of time. If you do *not* play The Dot Game, you will lose time and productivity on some questions, resulting in leaving a stack of easy questions unanswered. While you sit there stewing over Number 16, the clock is ticking away. Worse, your chances of getting Number 16 correct are going down because your anxiety level is going up. Do not do that. Just play The Dot Game as directed, and keep your forward progress moving.

There are some students who are simply slow readers or have difficulty with reading comprehension. This is often particularly true for test takers whose first language is not English. In these cases, The Dot Game is particularly beneficial. This test is long, has a lot of reading, and necessitates excellent comprehension skills. If you do not totally understand what is being asked, how can you expect to pick the right answer? Therefore, I strongly suggest that if you are a slow reader or if you have issues with reading comprehension that you check in to getting some help right away. Don't wait till the week of the test when there is little that can be done. Try talking to a reading teacher for suggestions and then follow them. Another good idea is to take a reading comprehension or speed-reading course through community education, a local community college, or online. Regardless, it is *imperative* that you play The Dot Game to keep you moving and focused. You do not want to run out of time while you are still trying to figure out the second decision set.

Last, in the unlikely event that you have played The Dot Game two or three times and for whatever reason you suddenly fall into a coma until a test monitor comes to shake you awake and tell you it is time to leave, here is what you do: Guess. Guess like crazy, and do it quick before they throw you out. Then go seek medical attention about your coma.

This is very important: There are no correct answers left blank. You must put *something* down to have a *chance* of getting it right. Any chance beats no chance, so guess like crazy. You are not penalized for wrong answers. You do get credit for correct answers. If you get it right due to blind luck, congratulations. Pick the most ideal response to create the most ideal situation. Remember to forget reality and to think ideal. The developers of this test want to know if you know how to lead a school in an ideal manner. That is the goal behind every question. Therefore, forget how you have seen someone else respond to a similar situation in real life unless that person was performing in an ideal manner. The number-one mistake people make on this test is to pick answers based on reality, things they have seen done in real life. Forget that. In response to every question ask yourself, "What is the most ideal response?" Once you have identified the most ideal response, you have the answer to the question even if it does sound Pollyanna-ish.

That, my friends, is how to play The Dot Game. It is deceptively simple. Play it and win. It will help you stay cool, calm, collected, confident, and almost downright cocky. More important, it will help you manage the clock and your stress and will help you ace this test the first time you take it!

THE DOG AND STAR GAME: A DECISION-MAKING STRATEGY

The 268 principal TExES exam is still largely a multiple-choice test. You do not need to memorize facts. You *do* need to be able to synthesize and apply the philosophy of the eleven competencies we discussed in Chapters 5 through 15 as well as the strategies presented here. There will be four answer choices. In the best of times, one of them will shout at you as being correct. That answer is a star. We like stars. They make our lives easy. Still, since you will be such a good test taker, you want to make sure you are right. Therefore, when you find a really good answer, otherwise known as a star, draw a little star by that response in your booklet. But keep reading. Do you see any more really good answers?

If so, mark them, too. By process of elimination, one of those stars has to be brighter than the other. That means, in truth, one is a star while another is a baby star, a twinkle. Think to yourself, if I can only pick one of these meteorites, which one will it be? Which one is the brightest? Which one has more language from the competencies in it? Which response includes the most Important Points to Remember as provided at the end of Chapters 5 through 15? That response is the star. Mark it.

While we love stars, there is another group of responses that we like just about as much. They are dogs. Dogs are *bad* answers. Why would we be watching for bad answers? Because there are only four response choices. If one of them is a dog, use those good old kinesthetic and visual senses again and *draw a great big line through it.* As you progress through the test, you will take great pride in drawing *big, heavy lines* through those dogs. This is important for three reasons:

1. Every time you identify a dog, your chances of getting the answer right go up by 25%.

2. If you can find a dog *and* a puppy, mark them both out. A puppy is another bad answer. It's just not quite as bad as the dog. But it is still wrong, and you know it is wrong. By marking out both a dog and a puppy, you increase your chances of getting the question right by 50%!

3. It is good psychology for you to *feel and see* the results of this decision-making process. It adds to your subconscious confidence that you are attacking the test in a systematic and methodical manner, and that you are going to *pass* this test out of sheer diligence and conscientiousness. Therefore, be sure to draw a line through every answer you know is wrong. It's good psychology and helps you select the right answer.

Let's say that out of four potential choices, you did not find a star. However, as you are reading the responses, you find a twinkle, or a pretty good answer. You are not in love with it, but it will do. You also found a dog and a puppy. The other choice is just . . . there. There is not much for or against it. Or, as often happens, it is a perfectly good response. It just does not answer *this* question. They do that a lot. It tends to confuse people who think, "That is a good thing to do." Well, it may be. Just because a response says George Washington was the first president of the United States and you know that is true, does not mean it is the correct answer for this question. Beware! They love to throw in distracters like that, which are totally true. Do not let them trick you! If a response does not answer this question, it is a *wrong* response even if it is a good thing to do. Always bear in mind what *this question* is asking. That is why it is important to *underline key words or phrases in every question.* It helps keep you focused on the *intent* of this question.

If you do not find a bright shining star, but you do find a twinkle, a puppy, a dog, and a nonissue, or distracter, your correct answer is the twinkle. It may not be an obvious meteorite like we love, but it will do. Mark it on your scrap paper. It is the best choice available and will get the job done. We love stars, and we love dogs. We will settle for twinkles and puppies. Each time you can identify any of these, your chances of getting the question correct go up by 25%. If you can eliminate two, your chances go up by 50%. There will be many times when you can eliminate all three wrong choices. By process of elimination you now have the correct answer. Mega kudos!

> All chocolate is good. The world revolves around chocolate. (Chocolate is a *star* answer! It takes nothing away from the Italian food. Italian food is still wonderful. By not selecting Italian food, we are not saying it isn't a good answer. It is just not the *best* answer. On the TExES exam, you are looking for the *best* answer or the *brightest* star. In this instance, chocolate is outshining Italian food, although not by much.)

KEY WORDS AND THEMES: "SHERRYS" REVISITED

Review Chapters 5 through 15 on the learner-centered competencies. You do not need to memorize them. However, read them over and over, slowly, for comprehension and synthesis of their concepts. Think about what they mean. Practice visualizing how you will put them into practice when you pass this test and become a principal. Go back and review Chapter 4, "Standing on the Promises," particularly focusing on the discussion on important recurring concepts and themes as presented in Figure 4.2. You will see key words and concepts repeated such as multiple uses of data for a concept and *all* and *facilitate* as words. Sometimes you will even see answer choices that appear to almost *quote* a competency. When you see answer choices that utilize the same words or concepts, pick that answer. If the test developers had liked other concepts, language, or words better, they would have used them. Stick with ideas you *know* they like. That is why they are in the competencies!

THE IDEAL PRINCIPAL

Let's review the concept of the ideal principal. The ideal principal always does what is right, even when it is difficult or politically unpopular. Think "ideal," then mark the ideal response. Collaborate with everyone on everything. Facilitate and align all students, teachers, parents, and everyone else for maximum productivity and efficiency to ensure continuous student success. You are the ideal principal. You are on a relentless pursuit of excellence for all school and community stakeholders. If all else fails, think, "Which one of these crazy choices would Elaine put?" Then mark it because it *is the right answer*!

SUMMARY

The Dot Game is a strategy to help you utilize your time effectively while also keeping your anxiety level down and confidence up. Use it. Repeat it till you have completed the test. However, if you have gone through the test two to three times and still have dots left, mark the responses you think the ideal principal would do. Remember, this test is not designed for what the average, run-of-the-mill principal would do. It is built on a philosophy that all principals want to do the *right, moral,* and *ethical* things necessary to produce schools that maximize student learning, productivity, and character for an improved democratic society. Do *not* select answers that you think are what is actually done in schools if there is a *better* choice that reaches to a higher standard of moral or ethical responsibility to the school community.

By playing The Dot Game and The Dog and Star Game as well as always thinking "ideal," you will make good choices and pass the TExES exam ASAP. Once you pass it, get your certification, and land a great job leading a school, remember that it is your moral and ethical responsibility to do the right thing even when something else is easier. Live the competencies. Let your walk match your talk for the benefit of every student. We are not in leadership for a quick or easy fix. We are in it to have a real impact on our world, to leave a legacy of unparalleled excellence, and to know when we go to bed at night that we have done every single thing we can to make those things happen. There has never been a time in the past when you have been needed more. Go forth, and do well. I believe in you, so always remember me, how I have advised you, and, please, keep me updated on all the wonderful things you are going to accomplish.

CHAPTER 18

Creating a Personal Success Plan

Where There Is a Will, There Is a Way

iStock/dszc

Try not to become a man of success, but rather try to become a man of value.

—Albert Einstein

You have goals of passing the TExES examination, obtaining principal certification, and becoming a great school leader focused on improving student performance. The first step in achieving these goals is passing this test. You have the necessary knowledge base from successful completion of your university or alternative preparation program. After reading, analyzing, and truly incorporating the concepts presented in this book into your leadership style, you will also have a solid understanding of the theoretical framework around which the test is constructed. The exam has been written to measure your understanding and capability of applying the eleven principal learner-centered competencies fully detailed in Chapters 5 through 15. Section III has also provided you with specific strategies to help you make correct decisions regarding scenarios on the exam. What else can you do to ensure you pass?

Two of Stephen Covey's *The 7 Habits of Highly Effective People* (1990) are

- begin with the end in mind, and

- sharpen the saw.

In preparing for what could possibly be the most important exam of your career, you need to do both. But, in simple language, what do these two habits mean, and how can you apply them in creating a personal plan for success on the principal TExES exam?

First, to begin with the end in mind means looking ahead to where you want to be (i.e., passing the TExES exam), then strategically calculating the exact things you must do between now and then to achieve it. Goals without deadlines are only dreams. Because of that, you must set a specific deadline for each thing you hope to accomplish in test preparation. Waiting till the last minute will not get you where you want to be. You will either run out of time before the test or end up in such a frenzied state that it will be increasingly difficult to make prudent choices of answers to questions and data analysis.

Similarly, as you reflectively and insightfully consider the exact things you need to do while preparing for the exam, you also will be sharpening the saw. Covey (1990) gives the analogy of lumberjacks in a contest to see who can chop the most trees. One lumberjack immediately starts chopping. Another takes his time and spends several important minutes calmly sharpening the blade on his saw. Bystanders likely thought he had not picked a fine time to take up saw sharpening.

However, once this lumberjack was convinced his blade was ready, he began to saw on a tree. Because his saw was sharper than the other fellow's, he was more efficient and effective cutting down the trees. He subsequently won the contest. The point is once we look ahead to what we need to accomplish before the exam, once we begin now (our test preparation planning process) with the end in mind (actually passing the exam), we must also analyze, procure, and implement the best tools and resources available to help us sharpen our saws to maximize their utilization.

Taking these things into consideration, stop now and seriously consider the following. Aside from my principal preparation program and this wonderful book:

- What other exact resources would be beneficial in helping you understand and best be able to apply the eleven principal competencies?

- Who can you talk to, or consult with, who has the knowledge, expertise, and wisdom to best help you understand and can apply the competencies in scenario-based problem solving?

- Who can you talk to, or consult with, who can share helpful organizational techniques that can benefit you in the data analysis section of the exam?

- Who can you talk to, or consult with, to help you with time and stress management as you prepare for the test?

- Who can you talk to, or consult with, to help you create and implement your own personal success plan?

- Once developed and implemented, what modification and accountability mechanisms can you use to enhance the plan and hold you responsible for following it?

Each of these is a serious question. There are no right or wrong answers. They will vary from test taker to test taker and situation to situation. Figure 18.1 shows a sample template to help you organize your planning process. Whether you use it, or something different, just make sure you use something. Write it down. Include a timeline and accountability system. Remember, in the end, wanting to pass the TExES exam is only a dream if you do not have a plan with a responsible timeline and accountability process.

FIGURE 18.1   Personal Success Template

Idea or Project to Address	Resources I Will Need	Projected Beginning Date	Projected Completion Date	Evaluation: How will I be able to measure what I have learned?	Accountability: How will I be held accountable?

TIPS FOR THOSE WHO HAVE NOT BEEN SUCCESSFUL ON THE EXAM . . . YET

For various reasons, sometimes a person will not immediately pass the test. Health, family, and stress issues are some reasons people do not pass. Because the test is long and involves a lot of reading, test takers who are slow readers, or who have poor reading comprehension skills, sometimes have difficulty. But the major reason people do not immediately pass is a lack of proper understanding of the eleven learner-centered competencies. If you fall in any of these categories, do not be discouraged. This is the longest and most reading-intensive TExES exam that currently exists. Developing and using a personal success plan such as the template provided in Figure 18.1 helps you create a concrete schema to help you succeed. Thus, the real issue becomes identifying the specific things you can do to improve your scores. If you did not do well last time, study your scores. Is there a domain in which you came very close to passing? If so, what are the things you can do to focus and improve in this area? The same is true for your lowest domain. Really focus on this area because it is dragging you down. Your lowest domain is your highest area of need. If you do not have much time to prepare, concentrate your attention on the chapters of this book that address your lowest area. Seek solid ways to increase your knowledge base and application skills in this area. Do not be afraid to ask school administrators to help you. Most of them will want to help you, but they need guidance on how to do it. If you can share with them your greatest areas of need, they can center their mentoring efforts in those areas.

THE "ELAINE WILMORE 5-C PLAN"

If you have truly studied, synthesized, and internalized the leadership concepts presented in this book, created and utilized a personal success plan, and sought assistance and mentoring in targeted areas from people you respect, you should do quite well this time. However, there are some additional things you can do to improve both your likelihood and confidence. You need the benefit of the "Elaine Wilmore 5-C Plan." The 5-C Plan consists of going into this test

calm,

cool,

collected,

confident, and almost downright . . .

cocky.

FIGURE 18.2   Utilize the "Elaine Wilmore 5-C Plan"

Denise Domingue

I have had *numerous* people from around the state say that prior to attending my preparation seminars or reading my books, they had been unsuccessful in passing the principal or principal TExES exam. Yet after *doing what I have stressed to them to do,* they passed their test. Hearing this kind of news never fails to make me happy. Actually, this kind of news, particularly from someone who had yet to be successful on one of the tests, really makes me smile from the inside out. Like everyone else, I am human. I get tired (real tired, actually), and even I can get worn down from the stress of life. Hearing from people who pass the test, hearing the joy in their voices, cards, letters, and email lifts me up more than you can ever know. Your success is important to me. I want you to pass this test. I want you to become the best principals our state and others have ever seen. Our kids deserve nothing less. Therefore, we have got to work together to get you through this test!

Here are some specific suggestions to help you do exactly that:

- Application of Competencies: Go back to each of the eleven learner-centered competencies. Read, study, and analyze them slowly for comprehension, not memorization, of the concepts they represent.

- Remember, the key here is *comprehension* of the concepts, not memorizing them.

- To help you comprehend and be able to apply their *meaning*, develop a portfolio with fifteen sections. There should be one section for each of the eleven competencies. Begin watching school-level administrators around you in various contexts. In your mind, try to associate every positive thing they do with at least one of the competencies. Take notes, collect artefacts, and write brief reflective summaries of each activity. Place the notes into the appropriate section of your competency portfolio. There is something about framing thoughts into logical sentences that helps us more fully understand what they mean. Otherwise, what could we write down? Writing the brief summaries will thus help you analyze the activity you have observed into its various components.

- Sometimes you will have difficulty deciding if an activity belongs with one or a different competency. That is all right. It probably does go both places. Do not stress over this. The principal's job is an integrated position. We are not going to split hairs over what goes where. You will not receive bonus points for knowing exactly which questions go with which competencies. *The important thing is that you are connecting real-life applications with the concepts of the competencies.* You are thus making the competencies come alive. You are internalizing and synthesizing them. When you see scenarios of principal behavior in the TExES questions or the data analysis section, you will already be accustomed to analyzing behaviors and making prudent organizational decisions. Your portfolio will help you select the appropriate responses. Your portfolio will be personal, authentic, and applied TExES preparation.

If you have taken the test before and not yet passed it look at your

- *Content Analysis:* Analyze the score sheet or sheets you have received in previous TExES endeavors. Write down your scores *per domain* rather than your total score. Forget your total score. If you bring up your domain and competency scores, your domain and competency scores will automatically bring up your overall score.

- *Personal Strengths and Weaknesses:* Within your scores, you will have relative strengths, which are your higher scores. You will also have relative weaknesses, which are your lower scores. Target the areas you would like to focus on for this test administration. Go back to your college textbooks and notes for those areas. Review them. Study particularly the corresponding chapters of this book that go with those competencies. Study the additional resources that I have suggested *per competency*. In this way, your preparation will be focused on *your* greatest needs. You will be working *smarter* rather than harder.

- *Reading Comprehension or Speed Reading Courses/Review:* I am convinced there are many highly intelligent people who have had difficulty passing various TExES exams due to a combination of factors. Some are not prepared cognitively. They do not have the appropriate knowledge base. Others have, amazingly, never had the *philosophy* of learner-centered leadership stressed to them. How can anyone be expected to pass a test if they do not have a comprehension of the theoretical framework on which it is built? Others are lacking in language and test-taking skills. Test takers whose primary language is not English sometimes have to work harder to ensure they understand the intent of the questions and responses.

Having someone with whom to do these activities collaboratively will multiply the benefits for both you and him or her. If you have an encouraging mentor, supportive friend, or even a friendly classmate, ask them if once a week they will take the time to sit down and let you walk through your portfolio with them. It will be particularly beneficial if your partner is preparing for the test, too. You can share your ideas, thoughts, and portfolios with each other, which will multiply the rewards. Orally describe each artefact, set of notes, and so forth, and then summarize how they apply to this competency and what you learned from them. The act of orally describing what something is and why you selected it will manifest itself in critical and reflective thinking. These are, of course, higher-order thinking skills, which is exactly what this test is all about. Benjamin Bloom would be proud. So will you when you get your passing TExES scores!

Some, though, have difficulty with TExES due to the immense amount of reading involved. Every decision set and question involves reading, comprehension, analysis, and synthesis for application. Although many of these people are smart and successful in life, reading comprehension is not high on their talent lists. Sometimes comprehension is not the only problem. Sometimes they read very slowly. Some are also slowed down because English is not their first language. It takes time to read in English, process and possibly translate what has been read into their primary language, then convert everything back to English to pick a correct response. All this takes time and time is not your friend. *I am your friend!* Do what I tell you to do! If you don't play the game my way, the clock could win instead of you. Once you start having to fight the clock, you're in trouble. Eventually, you may begin to panic. *We know for a fact that panic is counterproductive in passing the TExES exam and virtually any other high-stakes test.* When anxiety goes up, productivity goes down. That is not what we want. We want productivity to stay up and anxiety to stay down. Practice deep breathing or yoga relaxation techniques. I've never learned yoga, but I delivered three large babies by natural childbirth, thanks to the help of Lamaze breathing techniques. Believe me; those same Lamaze breathing techniques have served me quite well through the years when I have been stressed. In short, do whatever works to keep you calm as long as it is legal and moral.

If reading comprehension or speed is an issue with you, you already know it. There are various places, including Sylvan Learning Centers and university or school district continuing education courses, that offer classes in these areas. Another good resource would be local English, language arts, or reading teachers. They often know of many good books, tapes, or techniques that would be beneficial. Your public library, as well as school and university libraries, also have resources to assist you. I cannot stress enough the importance of reading comprehension in passing this test. If you think you read well, but have been unsuccessful in passing the TExES exam more than once, what on Earth do you stand to lose by seeking to improve your reading skills? Not only will it help you pass this test, it will also improve your quality of life in countless other areas.

TIPS FOR OUT-OF-STATE FUTURE TEXAS PRINCIPALS

Very often, there are people from out of state, particularly practicing administrators, who seek to become principals in the Great State of Texas. Welcome! We love our strong, independent state and welcome you to it. Be sure you bring along a firm commitment to learner-centered leadership and to improving student performance because that's what education in Texas is all about.

The competency information provided in this book will bring things you have known for years to the forefront of your mind. To my surprise, many of the states adjacent to Texas are not stressing learner-centered leadership. Or it could be that they are, but you have been out of school for a long time and not actively involved in this type of professional development. We can solve that.

It is particularly important for you to think "ideal principal." In many ways, it is more important for you than it is for the non-principals taking the test. Remember, this test is designed for *entry-level* administrative skills. If you have years of experience, you will have a tendency to look at potential responses from an experienced perspective. You know what will or will not work in real life.

Forget real life. Think *ideal.* If a response may seem a little *unrealistic* to you, but you know that in an *ideal school* with an *ideal principal* that is likely what would happen, *mark that answer*! It is the right one! The idea here is to lift the benchmark of principal behavior as much as possible, especially with new principals, to the level of ideal. Remember our pal Les Brown again. Aim for the moon. Even if you miss it, you will land among the stars. We want *every* principal, new and experienced, to aim for the moon, the very epitome of the ideal principal, every day in every way. In so doing, our schools may not reach the top, but they sure will achieve higher than they currently are. What on Earth could be wrong with that?

The last thing I suggest is for you to get on the Internet and study various Adequately Yearly Progress Reports and TAPR reports beyond the one I provided in Addendum B for various districts and schools. Since TAPR reports are a Texas thing, you may not be familiar with their layout. But you will be familiar with the types of data presented therein. Look up a TAPR report, and play with it. Assess them for the good, the bad, and the ugly. Design interventions that could potentially improve student learning. Becoming familiar and comfortable with TAPR and AYP reports prior to testing will save you time and anxiety on the day you test. You will be able to whiz right through it, playing The Dot Game, of course. Remember: *Think ideal.*

EVERYONE—TEXANS AND NON-TEXANS ALIKE

What else should you do to prepare yourself cognitively, psychologically, and emotionally?

Mantras

The administrative TExES exams are mind games based on implementing student-centered leadership. The domains and competencies develop and portray this philosophy. In this book, you have studied, processed, and applied them in every conceivable scenario. Cognitively you are prepared. Logically, you should and will pass the test.

What about illogically? What if you are so frightened that you cannot think straight? What if, deep down, you are truly scared you will fail the test? What if your job or future job depends on passing? You cannot think about being an ideal principal or developing an ideal school because you are too busy breaking out in hives.

You've got to break that paradigm. Your mind is the front wheel of the wheelbarrow that drives your life. Your mind must be convinced you will not just pass TExES, you will ace it. You will knock it dead. You will do so well that they will audit your results. You will do great! You will make me proud! Frankly, you will simply be amazing! People will look at you in awe!

To convince your inner self of that, begin at this moment saying out loud, "I am going to ace this test. I am going to do great. I am thinking 'ideal' all day long." Do this a hundred times a day from now until you pass. Write it on fifty sticky notes and put them everywhere. Each time you see one, read it out loud. Say it with spirit. Practice being calm, cool, collected, confident, and almost downright cocky! Repeat the mantra until you, and everyone around you, is sick of hearing it. Repeat it alone, in public, in boring meetings, in your car, while exercising or shopping. Sing it in the shower really loud. Repeat it until you drive yourself and others crazy. Repeat it over and over as you get ready and drive to the test. Keep repeating it as you take the test. You are what you believe you are. You are a success. You are going to make a real difference in this world. Believe it. Do it. You will be great!

FROM NOW TILL THE WEEK YOU TEST

From now till the test, review Section II of this book regularly. Put that in your personal success plan. Study the competencies. Read through them slowly as you focus on the concepts they represent. Do not attempt to memorize anything, but do focus on the terms, language, and common themes that emerge. Once a week, review Chapters 5 through 15. I do *not* want you to think, "Well, I read the book, so I am ready for the test." That is real nice, and you may pass the test. But you also need to prepare, integrate, synthesize, apply, and *not forget* all I have been preaching to you about these competencies.

By synthesizing the competencies over and over until you are sick of them and never want to see them again, you will become as familiar and comfortable with them and the concepts they represent as you currently are with driving to school. Driving to school may not be a big deal to you because you do it every day. But remember when you were first learning to drive? Driving *anywhere* was a big deal. You watched every corner, every traffic light, and likely gripped the steering wheel tightly when other cars came your way.

Think of these competencies as learning to drive. I want you so thoroughly familiar and comfortable with them that when you take the TExES, they will seem as natural as driving to school. You are the driver of this test. Drive it well.

THE WEEK YOU TEST

You have faithfully prepared. You have read Section II at least once a week until the week of the test. It is now time to get more intense. Reread the entire book. Focus this time on Section III with its strategies and techniques for success. Then *each night* before you go to bed, read through the competencies *again.* Do it as the last thing before you turn off the lights. Research says the last thing you have on your mind before falling asleep stays in your mind all night long. That is exactly where we want this information to be. We want it working its way through your mind while you sleep, eat, work, bathe, or fall into a coma.

As before, read for comprehension, not memorization. By reading the competencies many times, key words and phrases that appear on the test, especially in answers, will jump right out at you as if they were in bold print. That is good. Those are *stars*. Mark them. We know if the test developers had liked other words or phrases better, they would have used them. When they use their own language, they are *giving* you the answer. Take them up on it and say, "Oh! Thank you!"

Then send me chocolate, plain with no nuts, as a thank-you for clueing you in on all this. I don't like nuts in my chocolate because we already have way too many nuts in education. I also really like pink roses, just in case you wanted to know. There are no nuts in roses.

WHAT TO DO, AND NOT DO, THE NIGHT BEFORE THE TEST

The night before the test is like the last minutes of the test if you are still sitting there. If you are not familiar with the competencies and test-taking strategies presented here by that point, it is not going to come to you by osmosis or divine intervention. However, I have had more than one student promise me that prayer works. I am a big believer in prayer myself.

I pray for all my students before they test. From this point on, consider yourself my student.

In truth, this is what I want you to do. You will test on a Saturday. On the Friday before you test, come home from school or wherever and *relax*. Go out to dinner. Take in a movie that is *light* and fun with pure, mindless drivel. Do *not* go see anything stressful. You have enough stress in your life right now. You can see intense or stressful movies after the test when you are so relieved to have it behind you that you know that you could singlehandedly slay dragons. Think of it as a victory march.

But the night before the test, you want mindless drivel. You want *absolutely nothing stressful* going on. Talk to your family, assuming you have one, ahead of time. Make sure they understand the *importance* of you having a calm night. If the cat has kittens, let someone else tend to it. As far as I am concerned, I do not even want you to *know about it*. And if you win the Publisher's Clearinghouse, don't let anyone tell you until *after* this blasted test. Otherwise, it would be a distraction for you to think about how you are going to spend, invest, or give away all that money. After the test, you can celebrate and, of course, invite me.

On the night before the test, relax. Go out to dinner some place you like. Do something fun. Come home early. Take a nice, hot bubble bath, preferably with *peach* bubbles, in my honor, of course. Men, just take the bubble bath and hush up. Your wives will love it! You will become very relaxed, which is exactly the point.

Then go to bed. You may read through the competencies one last time. If you do not know them by now, cramming will not help. Read through them, turn off the lights, and say your prayers. The party is over.

WHAT TO DO, AND NOT DO, THE MORNING OR AFTERNOON OF THE TEST

Set your clock to get up in plenty of time, particularly if you are assigned a morning testing. I do not want you rushed and messing up all that good relaxation from last night. Have *plenty of time* to get ready and arrive. If necessary, get directions and practice driving the route to the testing site. Don't be late!

Eat something. Even if you are not a breakfast person, eat something anyway. Research shows people who have something in their stomachs to fuel their bodies perform better. We want you to have *peak performance.* This is Olympics Day for you. Don't you know all those athletes have specially designed meals to ensure peak performance? This is your Olympics. You may not have a nutritionist at your house, but you do have something loaded with protein. Avoid carbohydrates this morning. They may give you a quick rush, but by midmorning, your blood sugar will crash. Testing day is not the day for your blood sugar to crash. Eat protein instead. After the test, you can pig out on as many carbs as you want, but not now!

Dress comfortably and in layers. This may be the only time in your life that looking good does not count. Wear something comfortable. This includes your shoes. You do not need aching feet during the TExES examination. If you decide your feet hurt during the test, shed the shoes. If your feet tend to get cold when you are nervous, bring extra socks. Dress in layers. I have had *multiple* students around the entire state complain that the testing sites are really cold. If you dress in layers, you can shed some of them if you get too warm. There is nothing worse than being cold during a test. From the other perspective, some people respond to stress by getting really hot and sweating. Others respond by their blood pressure slowing down instead of going up. They get cold. By dressing in layers, you will be prepared for any situation. And last, if you have a lucky charm or talisman, wear it.

Arrive at the test site early. You do not want to be rushed or to take any chances with traffic, wrecks, emergencies, nuclear attack, and so on. There will be a large number of other test takers at your testing site. Most of them will *not* be taking the same test as you. The lengths of different tests vary, so do not be surprised or chagrined if people sitting around you get up and leave before you are anywhere close to being through. Do not assume that they are innately brilliant and that you are a bump on a pickle. That is not true. *You* are the one who is innately brilliant and *fabulously* well prepared. They may be taking a different test. Or they have guessed their way all the way through our test and are hoping for a computer miracle during grading. *You* stay focused on taking care of your own business. Do not worry about theirs.

Make sure you remember to play The Dot Game. It is such a simple strategy that you may be tempted to not do it. Do it anyway. It will save you both time and grief. It is a very good test-taking strategy to maximize your productivity. Both your body and your mind need this structure for addressing confusing questions. Review everything about The Dot Game the week of the test. Apply what you know. It is a well-seasoned game and has greater validity than the lottery. Utilize the Dog and Star Game. Work your way through the test two to three times using both strategies. Then hang it up. Remember, you do not have to make 100% on this test. All you have to do is pass it. Speaking as someone who has spent 15 glorious years serving on a public-school board, I can assure you that boards do not utilize TExES exam scores when selecting school administrators. You are well prepared for this test. You have answered every question. You have given it your all. You are done. Go home!

LIVING YOUR LIFE AFTER THE TEST

Celebrate!!!! Although most people think that they leave the testing site brain dead simply due to the length of the test, you will know in your heart that you passed this test. You will have a deep sense of accomplishment. You will feel an even greater sense of accomplishment the day you get your scores. But until then, there is not one more thing you can do except celebrate. You deserve it. If you want to see an action thriller tonight, go do it. If you want to run the Boston Marathon, go do it. If you want to eat your weight in chocolate, invite me. But whatever you do, do it because it is something that fills your soul with joy. You have accomplished a major goal. You have taken and passed the principal TExES exam. You may not have your scores yet, but you know something that the computer does not. *You won!*

Go forth and make every day of your life all it can be for yourself and others. Do something kind for a stranger. Make a difference in the life of at least one person every day. Change the world, one school at a time. Yes, I do realize that this sounds like a Pollyanna way to approach life and educational leadership. But our world has enough negativity and ugliness in it. We have terrorists, wars, poverty, hunger, abuse, disease, lack of respect for others with different opinions and perspectives; the list goes on and on. We are surrounded by it.

Let's be different. Let's do everything we can to fill the world with joy. Idealistic? Yes. Impossible? No, not if you will help me.

Will you come along?

SECTION IV

After You Pass the Test

That's What It's All About!

CHAPTER 19

That's What It's All About

Actually Becoming Certified

iStock/dszc

We make a living by what we get, but we make a life by what we give.

—**Winston Churchill**

Once you receive your passing scores in the mail, you can shout for joy, jump up and down, call your entire family and friends, toss young children in the air, shout the news to strangers on the street, *send me roses and chocolate*, and be quite proud of yourself. You have accomplished a very great thing! I can already tell you just how proud I am of you. Now, don't let me down! You must go out there and be the ideal principal that you have proven that you know how to be. I am counting on you to do exactly that.

FIGURE 19.1   First One, Now the Other

Michael Whitney

However, after the celebrating, there are a few things left for you to do to actually obtain your principal certification. You must pass the PASL, as described in Chapter 3. After that, it is your responsibility to officially apply for your certificate with the State Board for Educator Certification (SBEC) at www.sbec.state.tx.us. There is a certification fee, which you pay directly to them.

Your university, or alternative preparation program, will already have received your scores from the state. They will also be aware of your status with PASL. *After* you have passed these, gone to the SBEC website, applied for your certificate, and paid your fee, you should contact the certification office at your university or alternative preparation program. Their verification and endorsement of your application is required. However, they cannot go online to approve your application if you have not applied for it. That's why you must do the online application through SBEC *before* contacting your certification officer. Do not forget the order of these important steps. Without doing them, you will not become certified regardless of how many tests you ace. Many, but not all, universities and alternative programs will charge you a small processing fee for completing your certification paperwork. To avoid confusion, remember that this is a different fee from the one you paid SBEC for your actual certification.

If you are an out-of-state test taker and not directly affiliated with any Texas university or approved alternative provider, you will need to contact SBEC directly regarding your certification paperwork.

During the time that it takes SBEC to process your paperwork, you are not yet officially certified. However, you are *certifiable*. This means you *are* eligible to be employed as a certified principal. The school district may require you to present evidence that you have completed all program requirements including passing your TExES exam. This is something your university will be pleased to provide. Usually, a simple letter on official university (or alternative program) letterhead stating your status will suffice. Certifications are now provided online so both you and your school can see when your actual certification is finalized. It is a wonderful thing when you see your certification appear by your name online. Print it out, and show it off to everyone you see. Tell them how hard you worked to get that piece of paper and how much you *really* love me for helping you get it. It's your job to make me famous, but that won't be on the TExES exam.

KNOCK THE TOP OUT OF IT!

With today's critical shortage of certified administrators, you could very well be hired as a principal before your certification becomes official. In fact, it is entirely possible that you could be hired before you even take the test. Regardless, you still must take the test. Having the job before you are certified does not exempt you from taking and passing the

TExES exam. If that happens to you, do not blow off the test. It is still very serious to your career. Make sure you still study, prepare, and do every single thing I have told you to do to pass this test.

In the end, certification is more than a necessary step to your long-term employment as a school principal. Meeting all certification requirements through course work, practicums or internships, and the TExES examination are all designed for one purpose. *That purpose is to help you be the best principal on the face of this Earth.* Nothing less will do. Is it a competition to be the best principal? Of course it's not. We want each and every school to be absolutely outstanding. We want every teacher to be able to teach where each student can and will learn. We want every student to graduate equipped for success in life regardless if that means entering the world of work, the military, or higher education. We want every graduate to be an informed, voting citizen within a literate, free, and democratic society.

Until all this happens, we are not through with our work. We have not reached our destination where all schools and all society are ideal. Early in this book, I told you that I am the Pollyanna of school leadership. I reminded you that we already have enough educational cynics and do not need any more. Stretching toward the ideal may, or may not, be realistic. But it is absolutely necessary that you aim for it. If we don't aim for ideal, how will we ever make significant strides toward reaching it? Your part in this is to be the best principal your school, town, the Great State of Texas, and the world have ever seen. That is what it will take to change, improve, and enhance our global society, one school at a time. Let's start now with you.

Will it be a daunting task? Yes, it will. Will you become tired, frustrated, and totally disgusted with complicated, complex community, school, state, and federal politics? Yes, at times you will. But will this also be the most challenging and personally rewarding job you could ever imagine? Without a doubt it will be. There will be tears of fatigue and frustration, but there will also be tears of joy and elation. There will be times you want to beat your head against a wall or prefer to beat a few other people's heads instead. Yet there will also be times of jumping up and down internally and externally over something magnificent that has happened, something that those with lesser faith believed could not be done. Yet you knew that it could. They were the cynics while you were the idealist. You knew that good things *would* happen because there is nothing on this Earth that can make you give up in your continuing quest to change the world one school at a time.

You have now passed the TExES examination and are headed into your future with anticipation, hope, joy, courage, perseverance, and a little bit of fear. May every day of your journey to do what is right, to do what is ideal, to stay proactive, positive, and persuasive, be the best day imaginable. It is all before you now. Just reach out and take it. You've worked for it. You've earned it. It's yours. Just remember to send me chocolate and roses.

May you be forever blessed. Go forth, and make me proud. Make the world a better place. Together we *can* be the difference. Will you join me as we try?

Now, let's do it! Go knock the top out of this test!

Your friend and mentor now and forever,
Elaine L. Wilmore, PhD

Eternally grateful to be the daughter of my parents, the late Lee and Irene Litchfield of Port Arthur, Texas

Lee and Irene Litchfield

Addendum A

Chapter 149. Commissioner's Rules Concerning Educator Standards Subchapter BB. Administrator Standards

§149.2001. PRINCIPAL STANDARDS

(a) Purpose. The standards, indicators, knowledge, and skills identified in this section shall be used to align with the training, appraisal, and professional development of principals.

(b) Standards.

    (1) Standard 1—Instructional Leadership. The principal is responsible for ensuring every student receives high-quality instruction.

        (A) Knowledge and skills.

            (i) Effective instructional leaders:

                (I) prioritize instruction and student achievement by developing and sharing a clear definition of high-quality instruction based on best practices from research;

                (II) implement a rigorous curriculum aligned with state standards;

                (III) analyze the curriculum to ensure that teachers align content across grades and that curricular scopes and sequences meet the particular needs of their diverse student populations;

                (IV) model instructional strategies and set expectations for the content, rigor, and structure of lessons and unit plans; and

                (V) routinely monitor and improve instruction by visiting classrooms, giving formative feedback to teachers, and attending grade or team meetings.

(ii)   In schools led by effective instructional leaders, data are used to determine instructional decisions and monitor progress. Principals implement common interim assessment cycles to track classroom trends and determine appropriate interventions. Staff have the capacity to use data to drive effective instructional practices and interventions. The principal's focus on instruction results in a school filled with effective teachers who can describe, plan, and implement strong instruction and classrooms filled with students actively engaged in cognitively challenging and differentiated activities.

(B) Indicators.

  (i) Rigorous and aligned curriculum and assessment. The principal implements rigorous curricula and assessments aligned with state standards, including college and career readiness standards.

  (ii) Effective instructional practices. The principal develops high-quality instructional practices among teachers that improve student learning.

  (iii) Data-driven instruction and interventions. The principal monitors multiple forms of student data to inform instructional and intervention decisions and to close the achievement gap.

(2) Standard 2—Human Capital. The principal is responsible for ensuring there are high-quality teachers and staff in every classroom and throughout the school.

(A) Knowledge and skills.

  (i) Effective leaders of human capital:

    (I)   treat faculty/staff members as their most valuable resource and invest in the development, support, and supervision of the staff;

    (II)   ensure all staff have clear goals and expectations that guide them and by which they are assessed;

    (III)   are strategic in selecting and hiring candidates whose vision aligns with the school's vision and whose skills match the school's needs;

    (IV)   ensure that, once hired, teachers develop and grow by building layered supports that include regular observations, actionable feedback, and coaching and school-wide supports so that teachers know how they are performing;

    (V)   facilitate professional learning communities to review data and support development;

       (VI)   create opportunities for effective teachers and staff to take on a variety of leadership roles and delegate responsibilities to staff and administrators on the leadership team; and

      (VII)   use data from multiple points of the year to complete accurate evaluations of all staff, using evidence from regular observations, student data, and other sources to evaluate the effectiveness of teachers and staff.

    (ii)   In schools with effective leaders of human capital, staff understand how they are being evaluated and what the expectations are for their performance. Staff can identify areas of strength and have opportunities to practice and receive feedback on growth areas from the leadership team and peers. Staff evaluation data show variation based on effectiveness but also show improvement across years as development and retention efforts take effect. Across the school, staff support each other's development through regular opportunities for collaboration, and effective staff have access to a variety of leadership roles in the school.

(B)   Indicators.

    (i)   Targeted selection, placement, and retention. The principal selects, places, and retains effective teachers and staff.

    (ii)   Tailored development, feedback, and coaching. The principal coaches and develops teachers by giving individualized feedback and aligned professional development opportunities.

    (iii)   Staff collaboration and leadership. The principal implements collaborative structures and provides leadership opportunities for effective teachers and staff.

    (iv)   Systematic evaluation and supervision. The principal conducts rigorous evaluations of all staff using multiple data sources.

(3)   Standard 3—Executive Leadership. The principal is responsible for modeling a consistent focus on and commitment to improving student learning.

    (A)   Knowledge and skills.

      (i)   Effective executive leaders:

         (I)   are committed to ensuring the success of the school;

         (II)   motivate the school community by modeling a relentless pursuit of excellence;

(III) are reflective in their practice and strive to continually improve, learn, and grow;

(IV) view unsuccessful experiences as learning opportunities, remaining focused on solutions, and are not stymied by challenges or setbacks. When a strategy fails, these principals analyze data, assess implementation, and talk with stakeholders to understand what went wrong and how to adapt strategies moving forward;

(V) keep staff inspired and focused on the end goal even as they support effective change management;

(VI) have strong communication skills and understand how to communicate a message in different ways to meet the needs of various audiences;

(VII) are willing to listen to others and create opportunities for staff and stakeholders to provide feedback; and

(VIII) treat all members of the community with respect and develop strong, positive relationships with them.

(ii) In schools with effective executive leaders, teachers and staff are motivated and committed to excellence. They are vested in the school's improvement and participate in candid discussions of progress and challenges. They are comfortable providing feedback to the principal and other school leaders in pursuit of ongoing improvement, and they welcome feedback from students' families in support of improved student outcomes.

(B) Indicators.

(i) Resiliency and change management. The principal remains solutions-oriented, treats challenges as opportunities, and supports staff through changes.

(ii) Commitment to ongoing learning. The principal proactively seeks and acts on feedback, reflects on personal growth areas and seeks development opportunities, and accepts responsibility for mistakes.

(iii) Communication and interpersonal skills. The principal tailors communication strategies to the audience and develops meaningful and positive relationships.

(iv) Ethical behavior. The principal adheres to the educators' code of ethics in §247.2 of this title (relating to Code of Ethics and Standard Practices for Texas Educators), including following policies and procedures at his or her respective district.

(4) Standard 4—School Culture. The principal is responsible for establishing and implementing a shared vision and culture of high expectations for all staff and students.

(A) Knowledge and skills.

    (i) Effective culture leaders:

        (I) leverage school culture to drive improved outcomes and create high expectations;

        (II) establish and implement a shared vision of high achievement for all students and use that vision as the foundation for key decisions and priorities for the school;

        (III) establish and communicate consistent expectations for staff and students, providing supportive feedback to ensure a positive campus environment;

        (IV) focus on students' social and emotional development and help students develop resiliency and self-advocacy skills; and

        (V) treat families as key partners to support student learning, creating structures for two-way communication and regular updates on student progress. Regular opportunities exist for both families and the community to engage with the school and participate in school functions.

    (ii) In schools with effective culture leaders, staff believe in and are inspired by the school vision and have high expectations for all students. Staff take responsibility for communicating the vision in their classrooms and for implementing behavioral expectations throughout the building, not only in their own classrooms. Teachers regularly communicate with the families of their students to provide updates on progress and actively work with families to support learning at home. Members of the broader community regularly engage with the school community.

(B) Indicators.

    (i) Shared vision of high achievement. The principal develops and implements a shared vision of high expectations for students and staff.

    (ii) Culture of high expectations. The principal establishes and monitors clear expectations for adult and student conduct and implements social and emotional supports for students.

    (iii) Intentional family and community engagement. The principal engages families and community members in student learning.

(iv) Safe school environment. The principal creates an atmosphere of safety that encourages the social, emotional, and physical well-being of staff and students.

(v) Discipline. The principal oversees an orderly environment, maintaining expectations for student behavior while implementing a variety of student discipline techniques to meet the needs of individual students.

(5) Standard 5—Strategic Operations. The principal is responsible for implementing systems that align with the school's vision and improve the quality of instruction.

(A) Knowledge and skills.

(i) Effective leaders of strategic operations:

(I) assess the current needs of their schools, reviewing a wide set of evidence to determine the schools' priorities and set ambitious and measurable school goals, targets, and strategies that form the schools' strategic plans;

(II) with their leadership teams, regularly monitor multiple data points to evaluate progress toward goals, adjusting strategies that are proving ineffective;

(III) develop a year-long calendar and a daily schedule that strategically use time to both maximize instructional time and to create regular time for teacher collaboration and data review;

(IV) are deliberate in the allocation of resources (e.g., staff time, dollars, and tools), aligning them to the school priorities and goals, and work to access additional resources as needed to support learning; and

(V) treat central office staff as partners in achieving goals and collaborate with staff throughout the district to adapt policies as needed to meet the needs of students and staff.

(ii) In schools with effective leaders of strategic operations, staff have access to resources needed to meet the needs of all students. Staff understand the goals and expectations for students, have clear strategies for meeting those goals, and have the capacity to track progress. Members of the staff collaborate with the principal to develop the school calendar. Teacher teams and administrator teams meet regularly to review and improve instructional strategies and analyze student data. Throughout the year, all staff participate in formal development opportunities that build the capacity to identify and implement strategies aligned to the school's improvement goals.

(B)   Indicators.

(i)   Strategic planning. The principal outlines and tracks clear goals, targets, and strategies aligned to a school vision that improves teacher effectiveness and student outcomes.

(ii)   Maximized learning time. The principal implements daily schedules and a year-long calendar that plan for regular data-driven instruction cycles, give students access to diverse and rigorous course offerings, and build in time for staff professional development.

(iii)   Tactical resource management. The principal aligns resources with the needs of the school and effectively monitors the impact on school goals.

(iv)   Policy implementation and advocacy. The principal collaborates with district staff to implement and advocate for district policies that meet the needs of students and staff.

Statutory Authority: The provisions of this §149.2001 issued under the Texas Education Code, §21.3541.

Source: The provisions of this §149.2001 adopted to be effective June 8, 2014, 39 TexReg 4245.

Addendum B

2016-17 Texas Academic Performance Report

District Name:

Campus Name:

Campus Number:

2017 Accountability Rating: **Met Standard**

District Name:
Campus Name:
Campus Number:

Total Students: 542
Grade Span: PK - 05
School Type: Elementary

TEXAS EDUCATION AGENCY
Texas Academic Performance Report
2016-17 Campus Performance

		State	District	Campus	African American	Hispanic	White	American Indian	Asian	Pacific Islander	Two or More Races	Special Ed	Econ Disadv	ELL^
STAAR Percent at Approaches Grade Level or Above														
Grade 3														
Reading	2017	73%	64%	**86%**	*	69%	89%	-	*	-	*	*	76%	*
	2016	73%	66%	**88%**	*	95%	89%	-	-	*	*	*	79%	*
Mathematics	2017	78%	71%	**82%**	*	56%	87%	-	*	-	*	*	71%	*
	2016	75%	64%	**78%**	*	81%	78%	-	-	*	*	*	68%	*
STAAR Percent at Approaches Grade Level or Above														
Grade 4														
Reading	2017	70%	59%	**87%**	*	95%	89%	*	-	*	*	*	76%	*
	2016	75%	66%	**76%**	*	67%	80%	*	-	-	*	*	52%	*
Mathematics	2017	76%	65%	**81%**	*	91%	80%	*	-	*	*	75%	74%	*
	2016	73%	59%	**78%**	*	60%	85%	*	-	-	*	-	67%	*
Writing	2017	65%	50%	**70%**	*	57%	77%	*	-	*	*	*	50%	*
	2016	69%	57%	**80%**	*	73%	84%	*	-	-	*	63%	59%	*
STAAR Percent at Approaches Grade Level or Above														
Grade 5 *														
Reading	2017	82%	76%	**83%**	*	59%	90%	*	-	-	*	*	67%	*
	2016	81%	73%	**91%**	*	79%	96%	-	-	-	*	71%	85%	*
Mathematics	2017	87%	80%	**85%**	*	71%	90%	*	-	-	*	75%	73%	*
	2016	86%	76%	**92%**	*	92%	94%	-	-	-	*	71%	94%	*
Science	2017	74%	70%	**78%**	*	47%	87%	*	-	-	*	*	69%	*
	2016	74%	67%	**85%**	*	83%	85%	-	-	-	*	71%	82%	*
STAAR Percent at Approaches Grade Level or Above														
All Grades														
All Subjects	2017	75%	68%	**81%**	47%	70%	86%	100%	*	*	79%	57%	69%	69%
	2016	75%	67%	**84%**	39%	81%	87%	*	-	*	82%	61%	75%	65%
Reading	2017	72%	64%	**85%**	*	76%	89%	*	*	*	80%	50%	73%	78%
	2016	73%	65%	**85%**	*	82%	88%	*	-	*	88%	52%	74%	*

TEA Division of Performance Reporting

District Name:
Campus Name:
Campus Number:

Total Students: 542
Grade Span: PK - 05
School Type: Elementary

		State	District	Campus	African American	Hispanic	White	American Indian	Asian	Pacific Islander	Two or More Races	Special Ed	Econ Disadv	ELL^
STAAR Percent at Approaches Grade Level or Above														
All Grades														
Mathematics	2017	79%	74%	**83%**	*	75%	86%	*	*	*	80%	65%	73%	78%
	2016	76%	69%	**83%**	*	80%	86%	*	*	*	75%	67%	77%	71%
Writing	2017	67%	58%	**70%**	*	57%	77%	*	-	*	*	*	50%	*
	2016	69%	61%	**80%**	*	73%	84%	*	-	-	*	63%	59%	*
Science	2017	79%	73%	**78%**	*	47%	87%	*	-	-	*	*	69%	*
	2016	79%	73%	**85%**	*	83%	85%	-	-	-	*	71%	82%	*
STAAR Percent at Meets Grade Level														
All Grades														
Two or More Subjects	2017	48%	36%	**40%**	*	26%	44%	*	*	*	50%	*	22%	*
	2016	45%	33%	**42%**	*	21%	53%	*	-	*	*	29%	27%	*
Reading	2017	48%	38%	**50%**	*	26%	57%	*	*	*	60%	25%	26%	*
	2016	46%	36%	**52%**	*	35%	57%	*	-	*	88%	29%	32%	*
Mathematics	2017	48%	35%	**47%**	*	36%	51%	*	*	*	*	40%	38%	*
	2016	43%	31%	**40%**	*	19%	51%	*	-	*	*	29%	28%	*
Writing	2017	38%	27%	**36%**	*	40%	36%	*	-	*	*	*	20%	*
	2016	41%	34%	**45%**	*	*	55%	*	-	-	*	*	22%	*
Science	2017	52%	42%	**39%**	*	*	47%	*	-	-	*	*	21%	*
	2016	47%	37%	**44%**	*	25%	56%	-	-	-	*	*	44%	*
STAAR Percent at Masters Grade Level														
All Grades														
All Subjects	2017	20%	13%	**23%**	*	7%	27%	*	*	*	21%	17%	14%	*
	2016	18%	11%	**22%**	*	10%	26%	*	-	*	36%	16%	13%	*
Reading	2017	19%	12%	**26%**	*	*	32%	*	*	*	*	*	15%	*
	2016	17%	12%	**26%**	*	15%	29%	*	-	*	63%	*	17%	*
Mathematics	2017	23%	13%	**24%**	*	13%	28%	*	*	*	*	*	19%	*
	2016	19%	10%	**19%**	*	8%	24%	*	-	*	*	*	11%	*

TEA Division of Performance Reporting

Page 2

District Name:
Campus Name:
Campus Number:

Total Students: 542
Grade Span: PK - 05
School Type: Elementary

		State	District	Campus	African American	Hispanic	White	American Indian	Asian	Pacific Islander	Two or More Races	Special Ed	Econ Disadv	ELL^
STAAR Percent at Masters Grade Level														
All Grades														
Writing	2017	12%	8%	14%	*	*	19%	*	-	*	*	*	*	*
	2016	15%	11%	24%	*	*	31%	*	-	-	*	*	*	*
Science	2017	19%	13%	16%	*	*	20%	*	-	-	*	*	*	*
	2016	16%	11%	15%	*	*	19%	-	-	-	*	*	*	*
STAAR Percent Met or Exceeded Progress														
All Grades														
All Subjects	2017	61%	59%	59%	*	60%	58%	*	-	*	*	*	60%	*
	2016	62%	60%	66%	*	62%	69%	*	-	-	*	*	61%	*
Reading	2017	59%	58%	59%	*	*	61%	*	-	*	*	*	54%	*
	2016	60%	59%	61%	*	61%	61%	*	-	-	*	*	54%	*
Mathematics	2017	64%	61%	60%	*	67%	56%	*	-	*	*	*	65%	*
	2016	63%	61%	70%	*	63%	76%	*	-	-	*	*	69%	*
STAAR Percent Exceeded Progress														
All Grades														
All Subjects	2017	19%	15%	18%	*	14%	20%	*	-	*	*	*	17%	*
	2016	17%	14%	18%	*	16%	20%	*	-	-	*	*	14%	*
Reading	2017	17%	15%	16%	*	*	19%	*	-	*	*	*	14%	*
	2016	16%	14%	17%	*	17%	17%	*	-	-	*	*	8%	*
Mathematics	2017	20%	15%	19%	*	21%	20%	*	-	*	*	*	19%	*
	2016	17%	14%	19%	*	15%	23%	*	-	-	*	*	20%	*
Progress of Prior-Year Non-Proficient Students														
Sum of Grades 4-8														
Reading	2017	35%	32%	43%	*	*	50%	-	-	-	*	*	41%	*
	2016	35%	28%	38%	*	*	45%	-	-	-	*	*	*	-
Mathematics	2017	43%	42%	32%	*	*	37%	-	-	-	*	*	*	*

TEA Division of Performance Reporting

District Name:
Campus Name:
Campus Number:

Total Students: 542
Grade Span: PK - 05
School Type: Elementary

TEXAS EDUCATION AGENCY
Texas Academic Performance Report
2016-17 Campus Performance

	State	District	Campus	African American	Hispanic	White	American Indian	Asian	Pacific Islander	Two or More Races	Special Ed	Econ Disadv	ELL
Student Success Initiative													
Grade 5 Reading													
Students Meeting Approaches Grade Level on First STAAR Administration													
2017	72%	66%	**72%**	*	44%	80%	*	-	-	*	*	52%	*
Students Requiring Accelerated Instruction													
2017	28%	34%	**28%**	*	56%	20%	*	-	-	*	*	48%	*
STAAR Cumulative Met Standard													
2017	81%	76%	**83%**	*	59%	90%	*	-	-	*	*	67%	*
Grade 5 Mathematics													
Students Meeting Approaches Grade Level on First STAAR Administration													
2017	81%	72%	**76%**	*	53%	84%	*	-	-	*	*	63%	*
Students Requiring Accelerated Instruction													
2017	19%	28%	**24%**	*	47%	16%	*	-	-	*	*	37%	*
STAAR Cumulative Met Standard													
2017	87%	79%	**85%**	*	71%	90%	*	-	-	*	75%	73%	*

District Name:
Campus Name:
Campus Number:

Total Students: 542
Grade Span: PK - 05
(Current Year ELL Students)

		State	District	Campus	Bilingual Education	BE-Trans Early Exit	BE-Trans Late Exit	BE-Dual Two-Way	BE-Dual One-Way	ESL	ESL Content	ESL Pull-Out	LEP No Services	LEP With Services	Total ELL
STAAR Percent at Approaches Grade Level or Above															
All Grades															
All Subjects	2017	75%	68%	81%	-	-	-	-	-	67%	92%	42%	*	67%	69%
	2016	75%	67%	84%	-	-	-	-	-	65%	65%	-	-	65%	65%
Reading	2017	72%	64%	85%	-	-	-	-	-	75%	*	*	*	75%	78%
	2016	73%	65%	85%	-	-	-	-	-	*	*	-	-	*	*
Mathematics	2017	79%	74%	83%	-	-	-	-	-	75%	*	*	*	75%	78%
	2016	76%	69%	83%	-	-	-	-	-	71%	71%	-	-	71%	71%
Writing	2017	67%	58%	70%	-	-	-	-	-	*	*	-	-	*	*
	2016	69%	61%	80%	-	-	-	-	-	*	*	-	-	*	*
Science	2017	79%	73%	78%	-	-	-	-	-	*	-	-	-	*	*
	2016	79%	73%	85%	-	-	-	-	-	*	*	-	-	*	*
STAAR Percent at Meets Grade Level															
All Grades															
Two or More Subjects	2017	48%	36%	40%	-	-	-	-	-	*	*	*	*	*	*
	2016	45%	33%	42%	-	-	-	-	-	*	*	-	-	*	*
Reading	2017	48%	38%	50%	-	-	-	-	-	*	*	*	*	*	*
	2016	46%	36%	52%	-	-	-	-	-	*	*	-	-	*	*
Mathematics	2017	48%	35%	47%	-	-	-	-	-	*	*	*	*	*	*
	2016	43%	31%	40%	-	-	-	-	-	*	*	-	-	*	*
Writing	2017	38%	27%	36%	-	-	-	-	-	*	*	-	-	*	*
	2016	41%	34%	45%	-	-	-	-	-	*	*	-	-	*	*
Science	2017	52%	42%	39%	-	-	-	-	-	*	-	-	-	*	*
	2016	47%	37%	44%	-	-	-	-	-	*	*	-	-	*	*
STAAR Percent at Masters Grade Level															
All Grades															
All Subjects	2017	20%	13%	23%	-	-	-	-	-	*	*	*	*	*	*
	2016	18%	11%	22%	-	-	-	-	-	*	*	-	-	*	*

140

TEA Division of Performance Reporting

District Name:
Campus Name:
Campus Number:

Total Students: 542
Grade Span: PK - 05
(Current Year ELL Students)

TEXAS EDUCATION AGENCY
Texas Academic Performance Report
2016-17 Campus Performance
Bilingual Education/English as a Second Language

		State	District	Campus	Bilingual Education	BE-Trans Early Exit	BE-Trans Late Exit	BE-Dual Two-Way	BE-Dual One-Way	ESL	ESL Content	ESL Pull-Out	LEP No Services	LEP With Services	Total ELL
STAAR Percent at Masters Grade Level															
All Grades															
Reading	2017	19%	12%	26%	-	-	-	-	-	*	*	*	*	*	*
	2016	17%	12%	26%	-	-	-	-	-	*	*	-	-	*	*
Mathematics	2017	23%	13%	24%	-	-	-	-	-	*	*	*	*	*	*
	2016	19%	10%	19%	-	-	-	-	-	*	*	-	-	*	*
Writing	2017	12%	8%	14%	-	-	-	-	-	*	*	*	-	*	*
	2016	15%	11%	24%	-	-	-	-	-	*	*	-	-	*	*
Science	2017	19%	13%	16%	-	-	-	-	-	*	-	*	-	*	*
	2016	16%	11%	15%	-	-	-	-	-	*	*	-	-	*	*
STAAR Percent Met or Exceeded Progress															
All Grades															
All Subjects	2017	61%	59%	59%	-	-	-	-	-	*	*	*	-	*	*
	2016	62%	60%	66%	-	-	-	-	-	*	*	-	-	*	*
Reading	2017	59%	58%	59%	-	-	-	-	-	*	*	*	-	*	*
	2016	60%	59%	61%	-	-	-	-	-	*	*	-	-	*	*
Mathematics	2017	64%	61%	60%	-	-	-	-	-	*	*	*	-	*	*
	2016	63%	61%	70%	-	-	-	-	-	*	*	-	-	*	*
STAAR Percent Exceeded Progress															
All Grades															
All Subjects	2017	19%	15%	18%	-	-	-	-	-	*	*	*	-	*	*
	2016	17%	14%	18%	-	-	-	-	-	*	*	-	-	*	*
Reading	2017	17%	15%	16%	-	-	-	-	-	*	*	*	-	*	*
	2016	16%	14%	17%	-	-	-	-	-	*	*	-	-	*	*
Mathematics	2017	20%	15%	19%	-	-	-	-	-	*	*	*	-	*	*
	2016	17%	14%	19%	-	-	-	-	-	*	*	-	-	*	*
Progress of Prior-Year Non-Proficient Students															
Sum of Grades 4-8															
Reading	2017	35%	32%	43%	-	-	-	-	-	*	-	*	-	*	*
	2016	35%	28%	38%	-	-	-	-	-	*	-	-	-	-	-

TEXAS EDUCATION AGENCY
Texas Academic Performance Report
2016-17 Campus Performance
Bilingual Education/English as a Second Language

District Name:
Campus Name:
Campus Number:

Total Students: 542
Grade Span: PK - 05
(Current Year ELL Students)

Progress of Prior-Year Non-Proficient Students
Sum of Grades 4-8

	Year	State	District	Campus	Bilingual Education	BE-Trans Early Exit	BE-Trans Late Exit	BE-Dual Two-Way	BE-Dual One-Way	ESL	ESL Content	ESL Pull-Out	LEP No Services	LEP With Services	Total ELL
Mathematics	2017	43%	42%	32%	-	-	-	-	-	*	-	*	-	*	*

District Name:
Campus Name:
Campus Number:

Total Students: 542
Grade Span: PK - 05
School Type: Elementary

TEXAS EDUCATION AGENCY
Texas Academic Performance Report
2016-17 Campus Participation

2017 STAAR Participation (All Grades)

All Tests

	State	District	Campus	African American	Hispanic	White	American Indian	Asian	Pacific Islander	Two or More Races	Special Ed	Econ Disadv	ELL
Test Participant	99%	100%	100%	100%	99%	100%	100%	*	100%	100%	100%	100%	100%
Included in Accountability	94%	94%	93%	100%	94%	93%	100%	*	50%	93%	96%	96%	84%
Not Included in Accountability													
Mobile	4%	5%	7%	0%	5%	7%	0%	*	50%	7%	4%	4%	16%
Other Exclusions	1%	1%	0%	0%	0%	0%	0%	*	0%	0%	0%	0%	0%
Not Tested													
Absent	1%	0%	0%	0%	1%	0%	0%	*	0%	0%	0%	0%	0%
Other	0%	0%	0%	0%	0%	0%	0%	*	0%	0%	0%	0%	0%

2016 STAAR Participation (All Grades)

All Tests

	State	District	Campus	African American	Hispanic	White	American Indian	Asian	Pacific Islander	Two or More Races	Special Ed	Econ Disadv	ELL
Test Participant	99%	100%	100%	100%	100%	100%	*	-	*	100%	100%	100%	100%
Included in Accountability	94%	94%	95%	90%	99%	94%	*	-	*	92%	97%	94%	100%
Not Included in Accountability													
Mobile	4%	5%	5%	10%	1%	6%	*	-	*	8%	3%	6%	0%
Other Exclusions	1%	0%	0%	0%	0%	0%	*	-	*	0%	0%	0%	0%
Not Tested													
Absent	1%	0%	0%	0%	0%	0%	*	-	*	0%	0%	0%	0%
Other	0%	0%	0%	0%	0%	0%	*	-	*	0%	0%	0%	0%

TEXAS EDUCATION AGENCY
Texas Academic Performance Report
2016-17 Campus Attendance and Postsecondary Readiness

District Name:
Campus Name:
Campus Number:

Total Students: 542
Grade Span: PK - 05
School Type: Elementary

	State	District	Campus	African American	Hispanic	White	American Indian	Asian	Pacific Islander	Two or More Races	Special Ed	Econ Disadv	ELL
Attendance Rate													
2015-16	95.8%	95.3%	**96.5%**	97.2%	96.8%	96.4%	*	*	*	96.7%	96.6%	96.4%	98.0%
2014-15	95.7%	95.4%	**96.4%**	97.4%	96.8%	96.3%	*	*	*	95.7%	96.3%	96.1%	96.6%

District Name:

Campus Name:

Campus Number:

Total Students: 542

Grade Span: PK - 05

School Type: Elementary

Student Information	——— Campus ———		District	State
	Count	Percent		
Total Students:	542	100.0%	6,749	5,343,834
Students by Grade:				
Early Childhood Education	0	0.0%	0.0%	0.3%
Pre-Kindergarten	22	4.1%	4.0%	4.2%
Kindergarten	88	16.2%	8.1%	7.0%
Grade 1	83	15.3%	7.7%	7.4%
Grade 2	97	17.9%	8.1%	7.6%
Grade 3	86	15.9%	7.9%	7.7%
Grade 4	79	14.6%	7.7%	7.7%
Grade 5	87	16.1%	8.2%	7.5%
Grade 6	0	0.0%	7.3%	7.4%
Grade 7	0	0.0%	6.9%	7.4%
Grade 8	0	0.0%	7.2%	7.3%
Grade 9	0	0.0%	8.6%	8.1%
Grade 10	0	0.0%	7.1%	7.4%
Grade 11	0	0.0%	6.1%	6.8%
Grade 12	0	0.0%	5.2%	6.2%
Ethnic Distribution:				
African American	12	2.2%	3.4%	12.6%
Hispanic	125	23.1%	42.1%	52.4%
White	371	68.5%	49.3%	28.1%
American Indian	4	0.7%	0.6%	0.4%
Asian	3	0.6%	0.4%	4.2%
Pacific Islander	2	0.4%	1.4%	0.1%
Two or More Races	25	4.6%	2.7%	2.2%
Economically Disadvantaged	206	38.0%	66.7%	59.0%
Non-Educationally Disadvantaged	336	62.0%	33.3%	41.0%
English Language Learners (ELL)	34	6.3%	19.9%	18.9%
Students w/ Disciplinary Placements (2015-2016)	0	0.0%	1.9%	1.4%
At-Risk	219	40.4%	56.1%	50.3%
Students with Disabilities by Type of Primary Disability:				
Total Students with Disabilities	41			
By Type of Primary Disability				
Students with Intellectual Disabilities	*	*	46.2%	44.5%
Students with Physical Disabilities	31	75.6%	29.5%	21.9%
Students with Autism	*	*	8.5%	12.5%
Students with Behavioral Disabilities	5	12.2%	14.3%	19.9%
Students with Non-Categorical Early Childhood	0	0.0%	1.4%	1.3%

District Name:
Campus Name:
Campus Number:

Total Students: 542
Grade Span: PK - 05
School Type: Elementary

TEXAS EDUCATION AGENCY
Texas Academic Performance Report
2016-17 Campus Profile

| Student Information | -------- Campus -------- | | District | State |
	Count	Percent		
Mobility (2015-2016):				
Total Mobile Students	42	9.5%	17.8%	16.2%
By Ethnicity:				
African American	2	0.5%		
Hispanic	2	0.5%		
White	37	8.4%		
American Indian	0	0.0%		
Asian	0	0.0%		
Pacific Islander	0	0.0%		
Two or More Races	1	0.2%		

Page 11

TEA Division of Performance Reporting

District Name:
Campus Name:
Campus Number:

Total Students: 542
Grade Span: PK - 05
School Type: Elementary

TEXAS EDUCATION AGENCY
Texas Academic Performance Report
2016-17 Campus Profile

Student Information

Retention Rates by Grade:

	Non-Special Education Rates			Special Education Rates		
	Campus	District	State	Campus	District	State
Kindergarten	1.5%	2.6%	1.8%	0.0%	5.4%	7.7%
Grade 1	1.2%	2.8%	3.8%	0.0%	8.7%	6.8%
Grade 2	3.9%	1.4%	2.4%	0.0%	3.1%	3.1%
Grade 3	0.0%	0.0%	1.6%	0.0%	0.0%	1.2%
Grade 4	0.0%	0.4%	0.8%	0.0%	0.0%	0.7%
Grade 5	0.0%	0.0%	0.4%	0.0%	0.0%	0.7%
Grade 6	-	0.0%	0.6%	-	0.0%	0.7%
Grade 7	-	0.0%	0.7%	-	0.0%	0.8%
Grade 8	-	0.0%	0.5%	-	0.0%	0.9%

Class Size Information

Class Size Averages by Grade and Subject (Derived from teacher responsibility records):

	Campus	District	State
Elementary:			
Kindergarten	22.0	20.2	18.8
Grade 1	20.8	18.8	18.8
Grade 2	19.4	18.3	18.9
Grade 3	21.5	19.3	19.0
Grade 4	19.5	18.9	19.0
Grade 5	21.3	22.3	20.9
Grade 6	-	19.5	20.4
Secondary:			
English/Language Arts	-	20.5	16.8
Foreign Languages	-	23.0	18.7
Mathematics	-	19.8	18.0
Science	-	22.0	19.0
Social Studies	-	21.8	19.4

District Name:
Campus Name:
Campus Number:

Total Students: 542
Grade Span: PK - 05
School Type: Elementary

TEXAS EDUCATION AGENCY
Texas Academic Performance Report
2016-17 Campus Profile

Staff Information	Count/Average	Percent	District	State
Total Staff	44.5	100.0%	100.0%	100.0%
Professional Staff:	39.4	88.5%	62.0%	64.0%
Teachers	33.0	74.0%	49.9%	50.0%
Professional Support	4.5	10.0%	8.2%	10.0%
Campus Administration (School Leadership)	2.0	4.5%	3.0%	2.9%
Educational Aides:	5.1	11.5%	10.5%	9.6%
Total Minority Staff:	4.1	9.2%	22.7%	49.1%
Teachers by Ethnicity and Sex:				
African American	0.0	0.0%	1.8%	10.2%
Hispanic	3.0	9.1%	13.8%	26.6%
White	30.0	90.9%	81.6%	59.8%
American Indian	0.0	0.0%	1.1%	0.4%
Asian	0.0	0.0%	0.2%	1.5%
Pacific Islander	0.0	0.0%	0.0%	0.4%
Two or More Races	0.0	0.0%	1.5%	1.1%
Males	1.3	3.8%	20.9%	23.7%
Females	31.7	96.2%	79.1%	76.3%
Teachers by Highest Degree Held:				
No Degree	0.0	0.0%	0.6%	1.2%
Bachelors	29.2	88.6%	81.2%	74.5%
Masters	3.3	10.1%	17.8%	23.6%
Doctorate	0.4	1.3%	0.4%	0.6%
Teachers by Years of Experience:				
Beginning Teachers	2.0	6.1%	4.9%	7.8%
1-5 Years Experience	8.2	24.8%	32.5%	28.0%
6-10 Years Experience	4.3	12.9%	19.5%	20.9%
11-20 Years Experience	11.3	34.3%	26.9%	27.8%
Over 20 Years Experience	7.2	21.9%	16.2%	15.5%
Number of Students per Teacher	16.4	n/a	14.3	15.1

District Name:
Campus Name:
Campus Number:

Total Students: 542
Grade Span: PK - 05
School Type: Elementary

Staff Information	Campus	District	State
Experience of Campus Leadership:			
Average Years Experience of Principals	26.0	17.9	19.5
Average Years Experience of Principals with District	26.0	10.4	12.2
Average Years Experience of Assistant Principals	17.0	15.9	15.7
Average Years Experience of Assistant Principals with District	17.0	5.6	10.1
Average Years Experience of Teachers:	13.4	11.6	10.9
Average Years Experience of Teachers with District:	10.2	7.1	7.2
Average Teacher Salary by Years of Experience (regular duties only):			
Beginning Teachers	$45,850	$48,352	$46,199
1-5 Years Experience	$47,844	$49,806	$48,779
6-10 Years Experience	$50,027	$51,514	$51,184
11-20 Years Experience	$53,312	$55,194	$54,396
Over 20 Years Experience	$60,718	$61,873	$60,913
Average Actual Salaries (regular duties only):			
Teachers	$52,704	$53,478	$52,525
Professional Support	$52,659	$61,189	$61,728
Campus Administration (School Leadership)	$72,057	$77,028	$76,471
Instructional Staff Percent:	n/a	62.4%	64.6%
Contracted Instructional Staff (not incl. above):	0.0	0.0	2,110.5

Texas Academic Performance Report
2016-17 Campus Profile

District Name:
Campus Name:
Campus Number:

Total Students: 542
Grade Span: PK - 05
School Type: Elementary

Program Information	Campus		District	State
	Count	**Percent**	**District**	**State**
Student Enrollment by Program:				
Bilingual/ESL Education	33	6.1%	19.9%	18.8%
Career & Technical Education	0	0.0%	32.0%	25.0%
Gifted & Talented Education	49	9.0%	9.7%	7.8%
Special Education	41	7.6%	9.2%	8.8%
Teachers by Program (population served):				
Bilingual/ESL Education	1.0	3.0%	9.1%	6.0%
Career & Technical Education	0.0	0.0%	5.3%	4.5%
Compensatory Education	1.7	5.1%	2.7%	2.8%
Gifted & Talented Education	0.5	1.4%	0.6%	1.9%
Regular Education	28.7	86.9%	71.4%	72.8%
Special Education	1.2	3.6%	8.2%	8.6%
Other	0.0	0.0%	2.7%	3.4%

Link to:
PEIMS Financial Standard Reports/
2015-2016 Financial Actual Report

'^'   Indicates that ELL rates at met or exceeded progress and exceeded progress include current and monitored students.
'*'   Indicates results are masked due to small numbers to protect student confidentiality.
'***'   When only one group is masked, then the second smallest group is masked (regardless of size).
'-'   Indicates zero observations reported for this group.
'n/a'   Indicates data reporting is not applicable for this group.
'****' Indicates that rates for Reading and Mathematics are based on the cumulative results from the first and second administrations of STAAR.
'?'   Indicates that the data for this item were statistically improbable, or were reported outside a reasonable range.

Addendum C

Texas Administrative Code, Code of Ethics

TITLE 19	EDUCATION
PART 7	STATE BOARD FOR EDUCATOR CERTIFICATION
CHAPTER 247	EDUCATORS' CODE OF ETHICS
RULE §247.2	Code of Ethics and Standard Practices for Texas Educators

Enforceable Standards.
(1) Professional Ethical Conduct, Practices and Performance.
(A) Standard 1.1. The educator shall not intentionally, knowingly, or recklessly engage in deceptive practices regarding official policies of the school district, educational institution, educator preparation program, the Texas Education Agency, or the State Board for Educator Certification (SBEC) and its certification process.
(B) Standard 1.2. The educator shall not knowingly misappropriate, divert, or use monies, personnel, property, or equipment committed to his or her charge for personal gain or advantage.
(C) Standard 1.3. The educator shall not submit fraudulent requests for reimbursement, expenses, or pay.
(D) Standard 1.4. The educator shall not use institutional or professional privileges for personal or partisan advantage.
(E) Standard 1.5. The educator shall neither accept nor offer gratuities, gifts, or favors that impair professional judgment or to obtain special advantage. This standard shall not restrict the acceptance of gifts or tokens offered and accepted openly from students, parents of students, or other persons or organizations in recognition or appreciation of service.
(F) Standard 1.6. The educator shall not falsify records, or direct or coerce others to do so.
(G) Standard 1.7. The educator shall comply with state regulations, written local school board policies, and other state and federal laws.
(H) Standard 1.8. The educator shall apply for, accept, offer, or assign a position or a responsibility on the basis of professional qualifications.

(Continued)

(Continued)

(I)	Standard 1.9. The educator shall not make threats of violence against school district employees, school board members, students, or parents of students.
(J)	Standard 1.10. The educator shall be of good moral character and be worthy to instruct or supervise the youth of this state.
(K)	Standard 1.11. The educator shall not intentionally or knowingly misrepresent his or her employment history, criminal history, and/or disciplinary record when applying for subsequent employment.
(L)	Standard 1.12. The educator shall refrain from the illegal use or distribution of controlled substances and/or abuse of prescription drugs and toxic inhalants.
(M)	Standard 1.13. The educator shall not be under the influence of alcohol or consume alcoholic beverages on school property or during school activities when students are present.
(N)	Standard 1.14. The educator shall not assist another educator, school employee, contractor, or agent in obtaining a new job as an educator or in a school, apart from the routine transmission of administrative and personnel files, if the educator knows or has probable cause to believe that such person engaged in sexual misconduct regarding a minor or student in violation of the law.
(2) Ethical Conduct Toward Professional Colleagues.	
(A)	Standard 2.1. The educator shall not reveal confidential health or personnel information concerning colleagues unless disclosure serves lawful professional purposes or is required by law.
(B)	Standard 2.2. The educator shall not harm others by knowingly making false statements about a colleague or the school system.
(C)	Standard 2.3. The educator shall adhere to written local school board policies and state and federal laws regarding the hiring, evaluation, and dismissal of personnel.
(D)	Standard 2.4. The educator shall not interfere with a colleague's exercise of political, professional, or citizenship rights and responsibilities.
(E)	Standard 2.5. The educator shall not discriminate against or coerce a colleague on the basis of race, color, religion, national origin, age, gender, disability, family status, or sexual orientation.
(F)	Standard 2.6. The educator shall not use coercive means or promise of special treatment in order to influence professional decisions or colleagues.
(G)	Standard 2.7. The educator shall not retaliate against any individual who has filed a complaint with the SBEC or who provides information for a disciplinary investigation or proceeding under this chapter.
(3) Ethical Conduct Toward Students.	
(A)	Standard 3.1. The educator shall not reveal confidential information concerning students unless disclosure serves lawful professional purposes or is required by law.
(B)	Standard 3.2. The educator shall not intentionally, knowingly, or recklessly treat a student or minor in a manner that adversely affects or endangers the learning, physical health, mental health, or safety of the student or minor.
(C)	Standard 3.3. The educator shall not intentionally, knowingly, or recklessly misrepresent facts regarding a student.

(D)	Standard 3.4. The educator shall not exclude a student from participation in a program, deny benefits to a student, or grant an advantage to a student on the basis of race, color, gender, disability, national origin, religion, family status, or sexual orientation.
(E)	Standard 3.5. The educator shall not intentionally, knowingly, or recklessly engage in physical mistreatment, neglect, or abuse of a student or minor.
(F)	Standard 3.6. The educator shall not solicit or engage in sexual conduct or a romantic relationship with a student or minor.
(G)	Standard 3.7. The educator shall not furnish alcohol or illegal/unauthorized drugs to any person under 21 years of age unless the educator is a parent or guardian of that child or knowingly allow any person under 21 years of age unless the educator is a parent or guardian of that child to consume alcohol or illegal/unauthorized drugs in the presence of the educator.
(H)	Standard 3.8. The educator shall maintain appropriate professional educator-student relationships and boundaries based on a reasonably prudent educator standard.
(I)	Standard 3.9. The educator shall refrain from inappropriate communication with a student or minor, including, but not limited to, electronic communication such as cell phone, text messaging, email, instant messaging, blogging, or other social network communication. Factors that may be considered in assessing whether the communication is inappropriate include, but are not limited to:
	(i) the nature, purpose, timing, and amount of the communication;
	(ii) the subject matter of the communication;
	(iii) whether the communication was made openly or the educator attempted to conceal the communication;
	(iv) whether the communication could be reasonably interpreted as soliciting sexual contact or a romantic relationship;
	(v) whether the communication was sexually explicit; and
	(vi) whether the communication involved discussion(s) of the physical or sexual attractiveness or the sexual history, activities, preferences, or fantasies of either the educator or the student.

Source Note: The provisions of this §247.2 adopted to be effective March 1, 1998, 23 TexReg 1022; amended to be effective August 22, 2002, 27 TexReg 7530; amended to be effective December 26, 2010, 35 TexReg 11242; amended to be effective December 27, 2016, 41 TexReg 10329.

References

Covey, S. R. (1990). *The 7 habits of highly effective people.* New York, NY: Simon & Schuster.

Texas Education Agency. (2006). *Texas Examinations of Educator Standards: Preparation manual: Principal. 068.* Austin, TX: Author. Retrieved from http://cms.texes-ets.org/files/4714/4976/3536/068_principal_prep_manual.pdf

Wilmore, E. L. (2007). *Teacher leadership: Improving teaching and learning from inside the classroom.* Thousand Oaks, CA: Corwin.

Suggested Additional Reading

This list is not intended to be an exhaustive guide but rather a source for supplemental reading that supports the concepts presented in the Principal TExES Exam. Many of these resources include content that is relevant to more than one domain.

DOMAIN I: SCHOOL CULTURE

Blanchard, K., & Johnson, S. (1981). *The one minute manager.* New York, NY: Berkley.

Blankenstein, A. M. (2013). *Failure is not an option: Six principles that guide student achievement in high-performing schools.* Thousand Oaks, CA: Corwin.

Barth, R. S. (2003). *Lessons learned: Shaping relationships and the culture of the workplace.* Thousand Oaks, CA: Corwin.

Boss, Suzie. (2017) *All together now: How to engage your stakeholders in reimagining school.* Thousand Oaks, CA: Corwin.

Carter, D. W. & White, M. (2016). *Leading schools in disruptive times: how to survive hyper-change.* Thousand Oaks, CA: Corwin.

Cherry, D., & Spiegel, J. (2006). *Leadership, myth, & metaphor: Finding common ground to guide effective school change.* Thousand Oaks, CA: Corwin.

Collinson, V., & Cook, T. F. (2006*). Organizational learning: Improving learning, teaching, and leading in school systems.* Thousand Oaks, CA: Sage.

Dewitt, P. M. (2017). *School climate; Leading with collective efficacy.* Thousand Oaks, CA: Corwin.

Eisner, E. W. (2005). *Reimagining schools: The selected works of Elliot W. Eisner.* New York, NY: Routledge.

Feinberg, W. (2006). *For goodness sake: Religious schools and education for democratic citizenry.* New York, NY: Routledge.

Fullan, M. (2001). *Leading in a culture of change.* San Francisco, CA: Jossey-Bass.

Fullan, M. (2005). *Leadership & sustainability: System thinkers in action.* Thousand Oaks, CA: Corwin.

Giancola, J. M., & Hutchinson, J. K. (2005). *Transforming the culture of school leadership: Humanizing our practice.* Thousand Oaks, CA: Corwin.

Glaser, J. (2005). *Leading through collaboration: Guiding groups to productive solutions.* Thousand Oaks, CA: Corwin.

Halstead, J. M., & Pike, M. (2006). *Citizenship and moral education: Values in action.* New York, NY: Routledge.

Hargreaves, A., & Shirley, D. (2009). *The fourth way: The inspiring future for educational change.* Thousand Oaks, CA: Corwin.

Harris, S. (2005). *Bravo teacher! Building relationships with actions that value others.* Larchmont, NY: Eye on Education.

Joyner, E. T., Ben-Avie, M., & Comer, J. P. (2004). *Transforming school leadership and management to support student learning and development: The field guide to Comer schools in action.* Thousand Oaks, CA: Corwin.

Kilmek, K. J., Ritzenhein, E., & Sullivan, K. D. (2008). *Generative leadership: Shaping new futures for today's schools.* Thousand Oaks, CA: Corwin.

Kochanek, J. R. (2005). *Building trust for better schools: Research-based practices.* Thousand Oaks, CA: Corwin.

Louis, K. S. (2005). *Organizing for school change.* New York, NY: Routledge.

McNeal, B., & Oxholm, T. (2009). *A school district's journey to excellence: Lessons from business and education.* Thousand Oaks, CA: Corwin.

Monahan, T. (2005). *Globalization, technological change, and public education.* New York, NY: Routledge.

Olssen, M., Codd, J. A., & O'Neill, A. (2004). *Education policy: Globalization, citizenship, and democracy.* Thousand Oaks, CA: Sage.

Preble, B., & Gordon, R. (2011). *Transforming school climate and learning: Beyond bullying and compliance.* Thousand Oaks, CA: Corwin.

Smith, M. L., Miller-Kahn, L., Heinecke, W., & Jarvis, P. F. (2003). *Political spectacle and the fate of American schools.* New York, NY: Routledge.

Sunderman, G. L., Kim, J. S., & Orfield, G. (2005). *NCLB meets school realities: Lessons from the field.* Thousand Oaks, CA: Corwin.

Williams, R. B. (2008). *Twelve roles of facilitators for school change* (2nd ed.). Thousand Oaks, CA: Corwin.

DOMAIN II: LEADING LEARNING

Alford, B. J., & Nino, M. C. (2011). *Leading academic achievement for English language learners: A guide for principals.* Thousand Oaks, CA: Corwin.

BenShea, N. (2006). *The journey to greatness: And how to get there!* Thousand Oaks, CA: Corwin.

Bjork, L. G., & Kowalski, T. J. (Eds.). (2005). *The contemporary superintendent: Preparation, practice, and development.* Thousand Oaks, CA: Corwin.

Blanchard, K., Zigarmi, P., & Zigmari, D. (1985). *Leadership and the one minute manager.* New York, NY: William Morrow.

Blankstein, A. M., & Houston, P. D. (2011). *Leadership for social justice and democracy in our schools.* Thousand Oaks, CA: Corwin.

Brock, B. L., & Grady, M. L. (2000). *Rekindling the flame.* Thousand Oaks, CA: Corwin.

Brower, R. E., & Balch, B. V. (2005). *Transformational leadership & decision making in schools.* Thousand Oaks, CA: Corwin.

Brubaker, D. L. (2006). *The charismatic leader: The presentation of self and the creation of educational settings.* Thousand Oaks, CA: Corwin.

Burrup, P. E., Brimpley, V., Jr., & Garfield, R. R. (2012). *Financing education in a climate of change* (11th ed.). Boston, MA: Allyn & Bacon.

Bush, T., & Middlewood, D. (2005). *Leading and managing people in education.* Thousand Oaks, CA: Sage.

Caposey, P.J. (2017). *Making evaluation meaningful: Transforming the conversation to transform schools.* Thousand Oaks, CA: Corwin.

Capper, C. A., & Frattura, E. M. (2009). *Meeting the needs of students of all abilities: How leaders go beyond inclusion* (2nd ed.). Thousand Oaks, CA: Corwin.

Carr, J. F., & Harris, D. (2009). *Improve standards-based learning: A process guide for educational leaders.* Thousand Oaks, CA: Corwin.

Carter, S. C. (2010). *On purpose: How great school cultures form strong character.* Thousand Oaks, CA: Corwin.

Cherry, D., & Spiegel, J. (2006). *Leadership, myth, & metaphor: Finding common ground to guide effective school change.* Thousand Oaks, CA: Corwin.

Collier, C. (2010). *Seven steps to separating difference from disability.* Thousand Oaks, CA: Corwin.

Creighton, T. B. (2007). *Schools and data: The educator's guide for using data to improve decision making* (2nd ed.). Thousand Oaks, CA: Corwin.

Datnow, A., & Murphy, J. F. (2002). *Leadership lessons from comprehensive school reforms.* Thousand Oaks, CA: Corwin.

Davies, B., & Brighouse, T. (2009). *Passionate leadership in education.* Thousand Oaks, CA: Corwin.

DePree, M. (1989). *Leadership is an art.* New York, NY: Dell.

Downey, C. J., Steffy, B. E., Poston, W. K., Jr., & English, F. W. (2009). *Advancing the three-minute walk-through: Mastering reflective practice.* Thousand Oaks, CA: Corwin.

Duncan, S. F., & Goddard, H. W. (2005). *Family life education: Principles and practices for effective outreach.* Thousand Oaks, CA: Sage.

Dunklee, D. R. (2000). *If you want to lead, not just manage: A primer for principals.* Thousand Oaks, CA: Corwin.

Dunklee, D. R., & Shoop, R. J. (2001). *The principal's quick-reference guide to school law: Reducing liability, litigation, and other potential legal tangles.* Thousand Oaks, CA: Corwin.

Dunklee, D. R., & Shoop, R. J. (2006). *The principal's quick-reference guide to school law: Reducing liability, litigation, and other potential legal tangles.* Thousand Oaks, CA: Corwin.

Dyer, K. M. (2000). *The intuitive principal.* Thousand Oaks, CA: Corwin.

Earl, L. M., & Katz, S. (2006). *Leading schools in a data-rich world: Harnessing data for school improvement.* Thousand Oaks, CA: Corwin.

Eckert, J. (2017) *Leading together: Teachers and administrators improving student outcomes.* Thousand Oaks, CA: Corwin.

Eller, J., & Carlson, H. C. (2009). *So now you're the superintendent!* Thousand Oaks, CA: Corwin.

Erickson, C. L., Morley, R. E., & Veale, J. R. (2002). *Practical evaluations for collaborative services.* Thousand Oaks, CA: Corwin.

Ford, B. A., & Obiakor, F. E. (2002). *Creating successful learning environments for African American learners with exceptionalities.* Thousand Oaks, CA: Corwin.

Fullan, M. (2005). *Leadership sustainability: System thinkers in action.* Thousand Oaks, CA: Corwin.

Glanz, J. (2014). *Action research: An educational guide to school improvement* (3rd ed.) Norwood, MA: Christopher Gordon.

Glatthorn, A. A. (2017). *The principal as curriculum leader* (4th ed.). Thousand Oaks, CA: Corwin.

Glatthorn, A. A., Boshcee, F., & Bruce, W. M. (2006). *Curriculum leadership: Development and implementation.* Thousand Oaks, CA: Sage.

Goldring, E., & Berends, M. (2009). *Leading with data: Pathways to improve your school.* Thousand Oaks, CA: Corwin.

Gregory, G. H., & Chapman, C. (2007). *Differentiated instructional strategies: One size doesn't fit all.* Thousand Oaks, CA: Corwin.

Hoy, W. H., & Miskel, C. G. (2012). *Educational administration: Theory, research, and practice* (5th ed.). New York, NY: McGraw-Hill.

Hoyle, J. H., English, F., & Steffy, B. (1998). *Skills for successful 21st century school leaders.* Arlington, VA: American Association of School Administrators.

Imber, M., & Van Geel, T. (2000). *Education law* (2nd ed.). Mahwah, NJ: Lawrence Erlbaum Associates.

Israel, S. E., Sisk, D. A., & Block, C. C. (2006). *Collaborative literacy: Using gifted strategies to enrich learning for every student.* Thousand Oaks, CA: Corwin.

Johnson, R. S. (2002). *Using data to close the achievement gap: How to measure equity in our schools.* Thousand Oaks, CA: Corwin.

Johnson, S. (1998). *Who moved my cheese?* New York, NY: Putnam.

Joyner, E. T., Comer, J. P., & Ben-Avie, M. (2004). *Comer schools in action: The 3-volume field guide.* Thousand Oaks, CA: Corwin.

Kaser, J., Mundry, S., Stiles, K. E., & Loucks-Horsley, S. (2006). *Leading every day: 124 actions for effective leadership.* Thousand Oaks, CA: Corwin.

Levenson, S. (2006). *Big-time fundraising for today's schools.* Thousand Oaks, CA: Corwin.

Love, N. (2009). *Using data to improve learning for all: A collaborative inquiry approach.* Thousand Oaks, CA: Corwin.

Love, N., Stiles, K. E., Mundry, S., & DiRanna, K. (2008). *The data coach's guide to improving learning for all students: Unleashing the power of collaborative inquiry.* Thousand Oaks, CA: Corwin.

Maanum, J. L. (2009). *The general educator's guide to special education* (3rd ed.). Thousand Oaks, CA: Corwin.

Madigan, J. B., & Schroth-Cavataio, G. (2011). *Mentorship of special educators.* Thousand Oaks, CA: Corwin.

Mandinach, E. B., & Jackson, S. S. (2012). *Transforming teaching and learning through data-driven decision making: Classroom insights from educational psychology.* Thousand Oaks, CA: Corwin.

Martin, L. C. (2009). *Strategies for teaching students with learning disabilities.* Thousand Oaks, CA: Corwin.

McLaughlin, M. J. (2008). *What every principal needs to know about special education* (2nd ed.). Thousand Oaks, CA: Corwin.

McTighe, J., & Arter, J. (2001). *Scoring rubrics in the classroom: Using performance criteria for assessing and improving student performance.* Thousand Oaks, CA: Corwin.

Metzger, C. (2006). *Balancing leadership and personal growth: The school administrator's guide.* Thousand Oaks, CA: Corwin.

Miller, J. P. (2006). *Educating for wisdom and compassion: Creating conditions for timeless learning.* Thousand Oaks, CA: Corwin.

Moore, K. (2005). *Effective instructional strategies: From theory to practice.* Thousand Oaks, CA: Sage.

Nicholls, G. (2005). *The challenge to scholarship: Rethinking learning, teaching and research.* New York, NY: Routledge Falmer.

Nicoll, K. (2006). *Flexibility and lifelong learning: Policy, discourse and politics.* New York, NY: Routledge.

Olsen, K. D. (2010). *What brain research can teach about cutting school budgets.* Thousand Oaks, CA: Corwin.

Osborne, A. G., & Russo, C. J. (2009). *Discipline in special education.* Thousand Oaks, CA: Corwin.

Peters, T., & Waterman, R. H. (1993). *In search of excellence.* New York, NY: Warner Bros.

Popham, W. J. (2010). *Everything school leaders need to know about assessment.* Thousand Oaks, CA: Corwin.

Poston, W. K., Jr. (2010). *School budgeting for hard times: Confronting cutbacks and critics.* Thousand Oaks, CA: Corwin.

Rebore, R. W., & Walmsley, A. L. E. (2009). *Genuine school leadership: Experience, reflection, and beliefs.* Thousand Oaks, CA: Corwin.

Reksten, L. E. (2009). *Sustaining extraordinary student achievement.* Thousand Oaks, CA: Corwin.

Robinson, V., & Lai, M. K. (2006). *Practitioner research for educators: A guide to improving classrooms and schools.* Thousand Oaks, CA: Corwin.

Sagor, R. (2005). *The action research guidebook.* Thousand Oaks, CA: Corwin.

Sagor, R., & Rickey, D. (2012). *The relentless pursuit of excellence: Lessons from a transformational leader.* Thousand Oaks, CA: Corwin.

Schimmel, D., Eckes, S., & Militello, M. (2010). *Principals teaching the law: 10 legal lessons your teachers must know.* Thousand Oaks, CA: Corwin.

Schmuck, R. (2006). *Practical action research for change.* (2nd ed.). Thousand Oaks, CA: Corwin.

Sergiovanni, T. J. (2007). *Rethinking leadership: A collection of articles* (2nd ed.). Thousand Oaks, CA: Corwin.

Shoop, R. J., & Dunklee, D. R. (2006). *Anatomy of a lawsuit: What every education leader should know about legal actions.* Thousand Oaks, CA: Corwin.

Smith, R. L. & Smith, J. R.. (2018). *Impact Coaching: scaling instruction leadership.* Thousand Oaks, CA: Corwin.

Sorenson, R. D., & Goldsmith, L. M. (2012). *The principal's guide to school budgeting.* Thousand Oaks, CA: Corwin.

Sorenson, R. D., Goldsmith, L. M., Mendez, Z. Y., & Maxwell, K. T. (2011). *The principal's guide to curriculum leadership.* Thousand Oaks, CA: Corwin.

Thomson, S. (Ed.). (1993). *Principals of our changing schools: Knowledge and skill base.* Alexandria, VA: National Policy Board for Educational Administration.

Thompson, S. J., Quenemoen, R. F., Thurlow, M. L., & Ysseldyke, J. E. (2010). *Alternate assessments for students with disabilities.* Baltimore, MD: Paul H. Brooks.

Tomlinson, C. A. (2017). *How to differentiate instruction in mixed-ability classrooms* (3rd ed.). Alexandria, VA: Association for Supervision & Curriculum Development.

Tomlinson, C. A., & Allan, S. D. (2000). *Leadership for differentiating schools and classrooms.* Alexandria, VA: Association for Supervision & Curriculum Development.

DOMAIN III: HUMAN CAPITAL

Abrams, J. (2009). *Having hard conversations.* Thousand Oaks, CA: Corwin.

Capasso, R. L., & Daresh, J. C. (2001). *The school administrator internship handbook: Leading, mentoring, and participating in the internship program.* Thousand Oaks, CA: Corwin.

Covey, S. R. (1990). *The 7 habits of highly effective people.* New York, NY: Simon & Schuster.

Denmark, V. M., & Podsen, I. J. (2000). *Coaching and mentoring first-year and student teachers.* Larchmont, NY: Eye on Education.

Fichtman Dana, N., & Yendol-Hoppey, D. (2008). *The reflective educator's guide to professional development: Coaching inquiry-oriented learning communities.* Thousand Oaks, CA: Corwin.

Jarvis, P. (2007). *Lifelong learning and the learning society: Requirements and provision.* Florence, KY: Routledge.

Johnson, R. S., Mims-Cox, J. S., & Doyle-Nichols, A. (2006). *Developing portfolios in education: A guide to reflection, inquiry, and assessment.* Thousand Oaks, CA: Sage.

Kee, K., Anderson, K., Dearing, V., Harris, E., & Shuster, F. (2010). *Results coaching: The new essential for school leaders.* Thousand Oaks, CA: Corwin.

Kise, Jane A. G. (2017). *Differentiated coaching: A framework for helping educators change 2nd edition.* Thousand Oaks, CA: Corwin.

Knight, J. (2007). *Instructional coaching: A partnership approach to improving instruction.* Thousand Oaks, CA: Corwin.

Montgomery, K., & Wiley, D. (2004). *Creating E-portfolios using PowerPoint: A guide for educators.* Thousand Oaks, CA: Sage.

Morel, N. J., & Cushman, C. S. (2012). *How to build an instructional coaching program for maximum capacity.* Thousand Oaks, CA: Corwin.

Osborne, A. G., Jr., & Russo, C. J. (2011). *The legal rights and responsibilities of teachers: Issues of employment and instruction.* Thousand Oaks, CA: Corwin.

Osterman, K. F., & Kottkamp, R. B. (2004). *Reflective practice for educators: Professional development to improve student learning.* Thousand Oaks, CA: Corwin.

Pellicer, L. O. (2007). *Caring enough to lead* (2nd ed.). Thousand Oaks, CA: Corwin.

Reiss, K. (2006). *Leadership coaching for educators: Bringing out the best in school administrators.* Thousand Oaks, CA: Corwin.

Showers, B., & Joyce, B. (2002). *Student achievement through staff development* (3rd ed.). Alexandria, VA: Association for Supervision & Curriculum Development.

Sparks, D. (2006). *Leading for results: Transforming teaching, learning, and relationships in schools.* Thousand Oaks, CA: Corwin.

Strickland, C. A., & Glass, K. T. (2009). *Staff development guide for the parallel curriculum.* Thousand Oaks, CA: Corwin.

Thompson, R., Kitchie, L., & Gagnon, R. (2011). *Constructing an online professional learning network for school unity and student achievement.* Thousand Oaks, CA: Corwin.

West, C. E., & Derrington, M. L. (2009). *Leadership teaming: The superintendent-principal relationship.* Thousand Oaks, CA: Corwin.

Whitaker, T. A., Whitaker, B., & Lumpa, D. (2000). *Motivating and inspiring teachers: The educational leader's guide for building staff morale.* Larchmont, NY: Eye on Education.

Williams, R. B. (2006). *More than 50 ways to build team consensus.* Thousand Oaks, CA: Corwin.

Wilmore, E. L. (2002). *Principal leadership: Applying the educational leadership constituent council (ELCC) standards.* Thousand Oaks, CA: Corwin.

Wilmore, E. L. (2004). *Principal induction: A standards-based model for administrator development.* Thousand Oaks, CA: Corwin.

Wilmore, E. L. (2007). *Teacher leadership: Improving teaching and learning from inside the classroom.* Thousand Oaks, CA: Corwin.

Wilmore, E. L. (2008). *Superintendent leadership: Applying the educational leadership constituent council standards for improved district performance.* Thousand Oaks, CA: Corwin.

Yendol-Hoppey, D., & Dane, N. F. (2010). *Powerful professional development.* Thousand Oaks, CA: Corwin.

York-Barr, J., Sommers, W. A., Ghere, G. S., & Montie, J. (2006). *Reflective practice to improve schools: An action guide for educators.* Thousand Oaks, CA: Corwin.

DOMAIN IV: EXECUTIVE LEADERSHIP

Blanchard, K., Oncken, W., Jr., & Burrows, H. (1989). *The one minute manager meets the monkey.* New York, NY: William Morrow.

Bolman, L. G., & Deal, T. E. (2002). *Reframing the path to school leadership: A guide for teachers and principals.* Thousand Oaks, CA: Corwin.

Burke, M. A., & Picus, L. O. (2001). *Developing community-empowered schools.* Thousand Oaks, CA: Corwin.

Chadwick, K. G. (2004). *Improving schools through community engagement: A practical guide for educators.* Thousand Oaks, CA: Corwin.

Daresh, J. C., & Lynch, J. (2010). *Improve learning by building community.* Thousand Oaks, CA: Corwin.

Deli'Olio, J., & Donk, T. (2007). *Models of teaching: Connecting student learning with standards.* Thousand Oaks, CA: Sage.

Epstein, J. L., Sanders, M. G., Sheldon, S. B., Simon, B. S., Salinas, K. C., Jansorn, N. R., et al. (2009). *School, family, and community partnerships: Your handbook for action* (3rd ed.). Thousand Oaks, CA: Corwin.

Fiore, D. J., & Whitaker, T. (2001). *Dealing with difficult parents (and with parents in difficult situations).* Larchmont, NY: Eye on Education.

Holt, L. C., & Kysika, M. (2006). *Instructional patterns: Strategies for maximizing student learning.* Thousand Oaks, CA: Sage.

Hoyle, J. R. (2002). *Leadership and the force of love: Six keys to motivating with love.* Thousand Oaks, CA: Corwin.

Killion, J. (2017). *Assessing impact; Evaluating professional learning* (3rd ed.). Thousand Oaks, CA: Corwin.

Krzyzewski, M., & Phillips, D. T. (2000). *Leading with the heart: Coach K's successful strategies for basketball, business, and life.* New York, NY: Warner Books.

Longworth, N. (2006). *Learning cities, learning regions, learning communities: Lifelong learning and local government.* New York, NY: Routledge.

McEwan, E. K. (2004). *How to deal with parents who are angry, troubled, afraid, or just plain crazy* (2nd ed.). Thousand Oaks, CA: Corwin.

Murawski, W. W., & Spencer, S. (2011). *Collaborate, communicate, and differentiate!* Thousand Oaks, CA: Corwin.

Pryor, B. W., & Pryor, C. R. (2005). *The school leader's guide to understanding attitude and influencing behavior: Working with teachers, parents, students, and the community.* Thousand Oaks, CA: Corwin.

Sanders, M. G. (2006). *Building school-community partnerships: Collaboration for student success.* Thousand Oaks, CA: Corwin.

Solomon, P. G. (2002). *The assessment bridge: Positive ways to link tests to learning, standards, and curriculum improvement.* Thousand Oaks, CA: Corwin.

Spears, L., Lawrence, M., & Blanchard, K. (2002). *Focus on leadership: Servant-leadership for the 21st century.* New York, NY: Wiley & Sons.

Townsend, R. S., Johnston, G. L., Gross, G. E., Lynch, R., Garcy, L., Roberts, B., et al. (2007). *Effective superintendent-school board practices: Strategies for developing and maintaining good relationships with your board.* Thousand Oaks, CA: Corwin.

Weiss, H. B., Kreider, H., & Labez, M. E. (2005). *Preparing educators to involve families: From theory to practice.* Thousand Oaks, CA: Sage.

DOMAIN V: STRATEGIC OPERATIONS

Bolman, L. G., & Deal, T. E. (2001). *Leading with soul: An uncommon journey of spirit.* San Francisco, CA: Jossey-Bass.

Brooks-Young, S. (2007). *Critical technology issues for school leaders.* Thousand Oaks, CA: Corwin.

Bruner, J. M., & Lewis, D. K. (2009). *Safe & secure schools: 27 strategies for prevention and intervention.* Thousand Oaks, CA: Corwin.

Covey, S. R. (1990). *Principle-centered leadership.* New York, NY: Simon & Schuster.

Covey, S. R., Merrill, A. R., & Merrill, R. R. (1994). *First things first.* New York, NY: Simon & Schuster.

Hoyle, J. (2006). *Leadership and futuring: Making visions happen* (2nd ed.). Thousand Oaks, CA: Corwin.

Hoyle, J. R., Bjork, L. G., Collier, V., & Glass, T. (2005). *The superintendent as CEO: Standards-based performance.* Thousand Oaks, CA: Corwin.

Kimmelman, P. L. (2006). *Implementing NCLB: Creating a knowledge framework to support school improvement.* Thousand Oaks, CA: Corwin.

Kouzes, J. M., & Posner, B. Z. (1998). *Encouraging the heart: A leader's guide to rewarding and recognizing others.* San Francisco, CA: Jossey-Bass.

Lovely, S. (2006). *Setting leadership priorities: What's necessary, what's nice, and what's got to go.* Thousand Oaks, CA: Corwin.

Meyer, L. H., & Evans, I. M. (2012). *The school leader's guide to restorative school discipline.* Thousand Oaks, CA: Corwin.

Miles, K. H., & Frank, S. (2008). *The strategic school: Making the most of people, time, and money.* Thousand Oaks, CA: Corwin.

Streshly, W. A., Walsh, J., & Frase, L. E. (2001). *Avoiding legal hassles: What school administrators really need to know* (2nd ed.). Thousand Oaks, CA: Corwin.

Sullivan, S., & Glanz, J. (2006). *Building effective learning communities: Strategies for leadership, learning, & collaboration.* Thousand Oaks, CA: Corwin.

Taulbert, C. L. (2006). *Eight habits of the heart for educators: Building strong school communities through timeless values.* Thousand Oaks, CA: Corwin.

Trolley, B. C., & Hanel, C. (2009). *Cyber kids, cyber bullying, cyber balance.* Thousand Oaks, CA: Corwin.

Winslade, J., & Williams, M. (2011). *Safe and peaceful schools: Addressing conflict and eliminating violence.* Thousand Oaks, CA: Corwin.

Worthen, B., Sanders, J., & Fitzpatrick, J. (2010). *Program evaluation, alternative approaches and practical guidelines* (4th ed.). New York, NY: Addison-Wesley.

DOMAIN VI: ETHICS, EQUITY, AND DIVERSITY

Banks, J. (2006). *Race, culture, and education: The selected works of James A. Banks.* New York, NY: Routledge.

Banks, J. A., & Banks, C. M. (2015). *Multicultural education: Issues and perspectives* (9th ed.). Hoboken NJ: Wiley.

Bender, W. N. (2012). *Differentiating instruction for students with learning disabilities: New best practices for general and special educators.* Thousand Oaks, CA: Corwin.

Blanchard, K., & Peale, N. V. (1988). *The power of ethical management.* New York, NY: William Morrow.

Browne, J. R., II. (2012). *Walking the equity talk: A guide for culturally courageous leadership in school communities.* Thousand Oaks, CA: Corwin.

Bucher, R. D. (2014). *Diversity consciousness: Opening our minds to people, cultures, and opportunities.* (4th ed.). Upper Saddle River, NJ: Prentice Hall.

Burton, V. R. (2000). *Rich minds, rich rewards.* Dallas, TX: Pearl.

Calderon, M. & Slakk, S. (2018). *Teaching reading to English learners, grades. 6–12: A framework for improving achievement in the content areas* (2nd ed.). Thousand Oaks, CA: Corwin.

Cooper, J. E., He, Y., & Levin, B. B. (2011). *Developing critical cultural competence: A guide for 21st century educators.* Thousand Oaks, CA: Corwin.

Fullan, M. (2010). *The moral imperative realized.* Thousand Oaks, CA: Corwin.

Howard, T., Dresser, S. G., & Dunklee, D. R. (2015). *Poverty is not a learning disability: Equalizing opportunities for low SES students.* New York, NY: Skyhorse.

Houston, P. D., & Sokolow, S. L. (2006). *The spiritual dimension of leadership: 8 key principles to leading more effectively.* Thousand Oaks, CA: Corwin.

Kozol, J. (1992). *Savage inequalities: Children in America's schools.* New York, NY: Harper.

Kozol, J. (2000). *Ordinary resurrections: Children in the years of hope.* New York, NY: Crown.

Krovetz, M. L. (2008). *Fostering resilience: Expecting all students to use their minds and hearts well* (2nd ed.). Thousand Oaks, CA: Corwin.

Lindsey, R. B. (2017). *The cultural proficiency manifesto: Finding clarity amidst the noise.* Thousand Oaks, CA: Corwin.

Odden, A. (2012). *Improving student learning when budgets are tight.* Thousand Oaks, CA: Corwin.

Payne, R. K. (2005). *A framework for understanding poverty.* Baytown, TX: RFT.

Reagan, T. G., Case, C. W., & Brubacher, J. W. (2000). *Becoming a reflective educator: How to build a culture of inquiry in the schools.* Thousand Oaks, CA: Corwin.

Simpson, R. L. & McGinnis-Smith, E. (2018). *Social skills success for students with Asperger syndrome and high-functioning autism.* Thousand Oaks, CA:Corwin.

Singleton, G. E., & Linton, C. (2005). *Courageous conversations about race: A field guide for achieving equity in schools.* Thousand Oaks, CA: Corwin.

Strike, K. A. (2007). *Ethical leadership in schools: Creating community in an environment of accountability.* Thousand Oaks, CA: Corwin.

Terrell, R. D., & Lindsey, R. B. (2009). *Culturally proficient leadership: The personal journey begins within.* Thousand Oaks, CA: Corwin.

Tileston, D. W., & Darling, S. K. (2009). *Teaching students of poverty and diverse culture.* Thousand Oaks, CA: Corwin.

Walker, E., Sather, S. E., Norte, E., Katz, A., & Henze, R. C. (2002). *Leading for diversity: How school leaders promote interethnic relations.* Thousand Oaks, CA: Corwin.

An ideal principal
* knows students name
* knows parents
* working relationship with
   teachers
* go rapport w/community
* knows TEKS
* understands classroom
   struggles
* build morral
* positive & builds
   positive relationships
* Trust teahers
* problem solver
* has open door policy
* supports teachers,
   students & community
* coaches & encourages
* confidence builder
* understands the gaps
   in grade levels
* good listener
* enforces rules
* innovative
* supports teacher
   growth & understand
   needs for change.

Index

CORWIN LEADERSHIP

Anthony Kim & Alexis Gonzales-Black

Designed to foster flexibility and continuous innovation, this resource expands cutting-edge management and organizational techniques to empower schools with the agility and responsiveness vital to their new environment.

Jonathan Eckert

Explore the collective and reflective approach to progress, process, and programs that will build conditions that lead to strong leadership and teaching, which will improve student outcomes.

PJ Caposey

Offering a fresh perspective on teacher evaluation, this book guides administrators to transform their school culture and evaluation process to improve teacher practice and, ultimately, student achievement.

Dwight L. Carter & Mark White

Through understanding the past and envisioning the future, the authors use practical exercises and real-life examples to draw the blueprint for adapting schools to the age of hyper-change.

Raymond L. Smith & Julie R. Smith

This solid, sustainable, and laser-sharp focus on instructional leadership strategies for coaching might just be your most impactful investment toward student achievement.

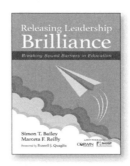

Simon T. Bailey & Marceta F. Reilly

This engaging resource provides a simple, sustainable framework that will help you move your school from mediocrity to brilliance.

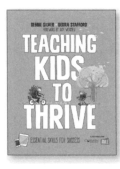

Debbie Silver & Dedra Stafford

Equip educators to develop resilient and mindful learners primed for academic growth and personal success.

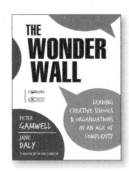

Peter Gamwell & Jane Daly

Discover a new perspective on how to nurture creativity, innovation, leadership, and engagement.

To order your copies, visit **corwin.com/leadership**

Leadership That Makes an Impact

Steven Katz, Lisa Ain Dack, & John Malloy

Leverage the oppositional forces of top-down expectations and bottom-up experience to create an intelligent, responsive school.

Peter M. DeWitt

Centered on staff efficacy, these resources present discussion questions, vignettes, strategies, and action steps to improve school climate, leadership collaboration, and student growth.

Eric Sheninger

Harness digital resources to create a new school culture, increase communication and student engagement, facilitate real-time professional growth, and access new opportunities for your school.

Russell J. Quaglia, Kristine Fox, Deborah Young, Michael J. Corso, & Lisa L. Lande

Listen to your school's voice to see how you can increase engagement, involvement, and academic motivation.

Michael Fullan, Joanne Quinn, & Joanne McEachen

Learn the right drivers to mobilize complex, coherent, whole-system change and transform learning for all students.

CORWIN LEADERSHIP

CORWIN

A SAGE Publishing Company

Helping educators make the greatest impact

CORWIN HAS ONE MISSION: to enhance education through intentional professional learning.

We build long-term relationships with our authors, educators, clients, and associations who partner with us to develop and continuously improve the best evidence-based practices that establish and support lifelong learning.